Praise fo

M000011996

A truly interesting and helpful combination of well-researched theory, vivid examples and down-to-earth practice. Written in a very accessible style, this book will help reassure you that, even in the darkest of times, you can get the brightest insights about yourself... and so do more than you ever imagined you could. RITA CLIFTON, CBE

Gone are the days of linear smooth career development and business growth. *The Rebuilders* teaches you to embrace change and step up to the occasion every time. This is a must-read for anyone keen to navigate and thrive in the uncertain world we live in. DR SARAH WOOD, OBE, DIGITAL ENTREPRENEUR, INVESTOR, AND AUTHOR OF *STEPPING UP*

Throughout my life, I have instinctively used failure, setbacks, prejudice and bigotry as fuel to drive me forward. Finally, we have a body of work in this book that can help us lean into such headwinds consciously and objectively. The lessons laid out within this book are universally relevant and immediately applicable. Brava team. This is a book to read, re-read and then read again. JONATHAN MILDENHALL, CO-FOUNDER AND CHAIR TWENTYFIRSTCENTURYBRAND, FORMER AIRBNB GLOBAL CMO

Loss and failure are inevitable on the road to success. *The Rebuilders* acts as a vital guide for anyone on that journey. CLIVE WOODWARD, ENGLAND'S 2003 RUGBY WORLD CUP WINNING HEAD COACH

The book is celebration of the bumps in the road as part of the journey. *The Rebuilders* gives an important and relatable insight into how to pick ourselves up after setbacks. An honest, enjoyable read! BRUCE DAISLEY, BESTSELLING AUTHOR OF *THE JOY OF WORK* AND FORMER TWITTER VP

At every turn I found myself thinking differently about certain situations at work, in life. It made my brain hurt in the best possible way. The perfect mixture of stats, science, stories, celebs and super-helpful tools to help us rebuild whatever mess we've got ourselves into. CAROLINE PAY, CCO (CHIEF CREATIVE OFFICER), HEADSPACE

What a clever and uplifting book, full of practical and informed advice on resilience and silver linings. DAME CILLA SNOWBALL

Now, more than ever, leaders need resilience, and this is a thought-provoking approach to building it. MARK READ, CEO, WPP

This is a modern-day Stoic's handbook, and all the more necessary and welcome for it. It is a book for anyone who has noticed the deep truth of John Lennon's line that 'Life is what happens to you while you're busy making other plans'. RORY SUTHERLAND, TED TALK SENSATION AND VICE CHAIRMAN OF OGILVY, AUTHOR OF *ALCHEMY, THE SURPRISING POWER OF IDEAS THAT DON'T MAKE SENSE*

The Rebuilders is a manual for survival in a chaotic world. How to define success? How to find certainty in uncertain times? And why ultimately adversity is a necessary ingredient in achieving any goal. Anna Vogt and Sara Tate explore human stories we can all learn from on our own quests to build the lives and careers we want. KATHRYN PARSONS, MBE, CO-FOUNDER OF DECODED

It takes courage and empathy, especially during a pandemic, to invest energy and time in giving back by creating a book such as this. The same courage and empathy that propels contemporary leaders to build a more human, equal and sustainable world. CRISTIANA FALCONE, STRATEGIC ADVISER, INVESTOR, PHILANTHROPIST

The authors have captured the zeitgeist in this book, reimagining the role that setbacks can play in moving the world forwards. We live in transitionary times, when work and life no longer follow predictable linear paths. This is a guide to navigating the new world of both chutes and ladders, showing us to how to learn and benefit from both life's ups and downs. A must read for anyone who wants to confront the reality of modern life and learn to thrive rather than survive! JAMES FOX, MD HEAD OF GLOBAL BRAND STRATEGY, GOLDMAN SACHS

The Rebuilders

Going from Setback to Comeback in Business and Beyond

Sara Tate and Anna Vogt

Kogan Page
INSPIRE

Publisher's note
Every possible effort has been made to ensure that the information contained in this book is accurate at the time of going to press, and the publishers and authors cannot accept responsibility for any errors or omissions, however caused. No responsibility for loss or damage occasioned to any person acting, or refraining from action, as a result of the material in this publication can be accepted by the editor, the publisher or the author.

First published in Great Britain and the United States in 2022 by Kogan Page Limited

Apart from any fair dealing for the purposes of research or private study, or criticism or review, as permitted under the Copyright, Designs and Patents Act 1988, this publication may only be reproduced, stored or transmitted, in any form or by any means, with the prior permission in writing of the publishers, or in the case of reprographic reproduction in accordance with the terms and licences issued by the CLA. Enquiries concerning reproduction outside these terms should be sent to the publishers at the undermentioned addresses:

2nd Floor, 45 Gee Street	8 W 38th Street, Suite 902	4737/23 Ansari Road
London	New York, NY 10018	Daryaganj
EC1V 3RS	USA	New Delhi 110002
United Kingdom		India

www.koganpage.com

Kogan Page books are printed on paper from sustainable forests.

© Sara Tate and Anna Vogt, 2022

The right of Sara Tate and Anna Vogt to be identified as the authors of this work has been asserted by them in accordance with the Copyright, Designs and Patents Act 1988.

ISBNs

Hardback	978 1 3986 0603 6
Paperback	978 1 3986 0601 2
Ebook	978 1 3986 0602 9

British Library Cataloguing-in-Publication Data

A CIP record for this book is available from the British Library.

Library of Congress Control Number
2022011673

Typeset by Integra Software Services, Pondicherry
Print production managed by Jellyfish
Printed and bound by CPI Group (UK) Ltd, Croydon CR0 4YY

To Rosamund, Iris, Joseph and Otto. May you grow up to embrace your comebacks as your ultimate successes in life.

Contents

List of figures and tables

Preface

So you're contemplating a rebuild, or you know someone who is rebuilding or you have picked up this book in the hopes of finding out how to re-hinge your toilet seat?

If you're looking for advice on any type of DIY, craftsmanship or similar, sorry to disappoint. If however, as the subtitle suggests, something has gone seriously off the rails at work or at home, this book is for you.

Having spent many decades working in advertising, reinvigorating brands that were falling behind their competitors, and most recently taking on a struggling global advertising agency and making it profitable again, we have learnt a thing or two about setbacks and how to turn them around. And just as we thought we had a handle on things, the Covid-19 pandemic struck. A whole new reality unfolded overnight and we discovered that many of the lessons we had learnt by working with clients in challenging business environments also applied to people coping with a challenging reality.

Which makes sense, because businesses are made up of people and in order to advertise effectively, you've got to understand how people think and make decisions. To delve further into this finding (and, in truth, to escape our children for a few hours each week whilst we were in the middle of home-schooling dramas and wiping down our groceries with anti-bacterial wet wipes) we decided to start a podcast dedicated to this discovery. But this time looking at it from the very personal, very human angle rather than the business end. The Rebuilders was thus born and we were blown away by the stories, the insights and the lessons we were learning. Not only because they were deeply moving and revelatory, but because they applied to so many other situations in life and work. A divorce can teach you how to revive a magazine, prison can help you sort out how to go about winning new business, cancer can help untangle sticky situations, and losing a rugby match can teach you how to smash a pitch. Every adverse situation is as unique as its owner, but the solutions can help many. Because resilience has the ability to connect us not just on a human level, but on a practical level, too.

Each chapter is an ingredient to rebuilding. It has made it into this book because it has applied to many people we have spoken to, in vastly different situations. It's an insight, a story, a tool, an inspiring anecdote to help you unpick your setback in a way that can move you forward successfully.

Read the whole book now, read a chapter later, or buy it and put it away for a rainy day. It is meant to be dipped in and out of, depending on the situation you are facing and the support you are looking for. One or more chapters might just offer a spark that helps you reframe how you are looking at your challenge and put it into a slightly different perspective.

This book was written in 2021 when many a rebuild was underway. The Covid-19 pandemic has forced most of us, in one way or another, to pick up the pieces of a relationship, sift through financial ruin, deal with health problems, fix business cultures that are falling apart, revive whole industries that have become seemingly obsolete, unlearn new habits that are unhelpful, same with old habits that have been exacerbated, and the list goes on and on. We all have our mountains to climb. Setbacks are one of life's most democratic experiences, and thus ones that connects us all and we can share. So instead of dreading them, feeling ashamed by them, running away and pretending they're not happening, let's make the most of them. And let's be proud that we were not defeated, but rather that we made something good come from a smelly pile of rubbish.

When life gives you lemons, rebuild.

PART ONE

Reframing your setback

CHAPTER ONE

When is a setback not a setback?

So often things that you regard as an impediment in life turn out to be a great good fortune. JUSTICE RUTH BADER GINSBURG (ECONOMY, 2019)

On **progress.** No one relishes a setback. The clue is in the name. We have plans that we want to progress with and setbacks seem to take us further away from where we want to be. But progress is rarely a straight line and this chapter explores how in the middle of things going wrong, things may actually end up going right.

> **Myth** – Setbacks send us backwards.
> **Truth** – Nothing moves us forwards faster than a setback.

Hearts get broken, businesses fail and plans veer off course. Setbacks happen. It's the way of the world. Sometimes we have a hand in them like the exam we didn't study for, the relationship we weren't committed to or the job we never really liked. But sometimes they happen to us. There we are trundling along when a recession, a global pandemic or an illness come crashing in out of nowhere. But don't worry it's not all doom and gloom because nothing has the power to move us forwards faster than a setback.

Myth

'In the long run we are all dead,' said the economist Maynard Keynes, now dead himself (Keynes, 1924). Even amongst economists who aren't known for their cheery outlooks, this seems like a pretty gloomy thought, but he had a point. He believed that long-term planning is a tricky beast, fraught with mishaps and that nothing stays on the up forever. As much as we would like to, it is impossible to see into the future and avoid the potholes that line our path through life and work. While economists and Eastern mysticism don't generally have much in common, Buddhism contains a similar belief. According to Buddhism, transience and suffering are universal characteristics of existence. Nothing is fixed or permanent, everything rises and falls, and suffering comes from trying to hold too tight to things that are transient and impermanent. There will be happy and joyful moments in life, but they won't last forever.

So the bad news is that setbacks are inevitable but the good news is that life is a series of cycles not a straight line. We shouldn't beat ourselves up when things go awry because nothing stays on top forever. And while some things are on the way down, others are on the way up. Businesses are launched, fortunes are made, people get married and illnesses improve. While nothing is ever always on the up, nothing is ever always on the way down. Nowhere is this cycle of change more visible than in business. No one wants to see their numbers going in the wrong direction but it is a fact that what got you to the top won't keep you there. Fifty-two per cent of the Fortune 500 companies from 2000 are now extinct and while the life expectancy of these companies used to be around 75 years, that horizon has shrunk to 15 (Berman, 2022). Leaders that factor this ebb and flow this into their decision making are likely to stay on top for longer.

Also as Ruth Bader Ginsberg says, it's not always clear at the time whether something is a good or a bad event. The real impact, positive or negative, is often only revealed much later. Sometimes the thing that went wrong leads to more things that go right. Hence the saying in comedy circles that 'comedy equals tragedy plus time'. How many occasions can you think of where an unmitigated disaster seems like a lucky break several months down the line? The job you didn't get led you to work in another firm where you met your future spouse. The failure of a business taught you what you needed for the next one to succeed. When Google launched Google Glass in 2013 the web-enabled glasses were so derided that early-adopters were nick-named glass-holes (source 4b). But far from being an all-out disaster, the technology went on to find valuable applications in industrial environments for the likes of engineers and technicians. Elements of Glass AR technology also evolved as the foundation for many consumer augmented reality products flourishing today (Gibbs, 2014).

There is another reason why setbacks might not be all they seem. We don't like things to go wrong because it upsets our plans and shakes our status quo. It makes us feel uncertain and insecure, not knowing what will happen or what comes next. Far more enjoyable to potter along in the comfortable equilibrium that we are used to. But equilibrium can also be dangerous. It can be a nice bath that we sit in while it gets slowly cold without us noticing. Trying to preserve our equilibrium can leave us stuck in positions and places that don't really suit us or serve us anymore. Staying still for fear of the repercussions of change may stop us even noticing that the bath is now stone cold. In business staying still can be a death knell. The urge to simply maintain equilibrium leads to incremental and protectionist thinking. It leads to breeding faster horses in the age of the car or Blockbuster ploughing ahead with the movie rental business while the woods were burning.

To better understand the human urge to maintain equilibrium and what happens when it is disrupted, we decided to explore the realm of relationships. Marriage and long-term partnerships are hugely painful and turbulent to leave, causing many people to stay in them long after they have ceased to be happy. Charlotte Friedman is a former family law barrister who transitioned to become a psychotherapist helping people to navigate the emotional journey of separation and divorce that she had witnessed in the courts for so long. By the time individuals or couples come to see her, their relationships are no longer bringing them happiness but, as Charlotte explains, they may be so accustomed to their situation that they become stuck. Her role is to see the current situation more clearly, to see 'whether the good outweighs the bad, or whether the bad is such that the good is insignificant when it comes to that point … to help move them out of a stuck position'.

We can become so accustomed to a situation that we don't see that the good has drained away. However, taking a decision to upset the equilibrium and change a familiar situation can be a terrifying prospect. We become so accustomed to managing where we are and how we feel, even if things aren't hunky dory, that we become stuck. To make a change means creating instability, having to figure out what comes next and dealing with a truck load of new and unforeseen challenges. For many people in relationships this holds them in the status quo.

> It's very, very scary [for people]. How to manage it, is to be
> able to think are you more attached to this not very pleasant
> way of living? More than the freedom of something new?
> Although you don't know what the new is. Because being free
> is frightening, but it's so incredibly exciting and very creative.
> '[People think] I just don't know. I don't know where I'm
> going to go, what I'm going to do, what life will look like.'
> People need to separate from a bit of themselves that is very
> attached to the status quo in order to separate from something
> which makes them unhappy., because our equilibrium is really
> maintained by maintaining the status quo.

7

Charlotte's work is to help people understand this process and support them in stepping into what might come next.

As well as highlighting how difficult it can be to break out of our equilibrium even when it is no longer serving us, Charlotte's work also shows the positives that change can bring. By the time the discomfort of their current situation has led people to see Charlotte, almost any change can be a good thing. Separating might be the right solution but those that stay together can also see improvements.

> Couples can stay together, if they can use the things that aren't so great to develop, to get past it and have proper conversations, rather than living in a very accusatory, fault-finding repetitive cycle. If both people have enough insight and the ability to reflect on their own behaviour, you can really develop and grow a much better relationship.

Reconcile or separate, the choice doesn't matter as much as the fact that some change, any change, is preferable to the current unhappy stasis.

This exploration of what it takes to leave or make changes to a long endured situation, highlights as important learning. Namely that things going badly is sometimes a prerequisite for things going better. Without things coming to a head, Charlotte's clients may never come to see her nor feel the need to upset their equilibrium and enact change. Whether to stay and address what needs mending in the current situation, or to move on and rebuild afresh, a level of discomfort spurs the change. Setbacks might be painful and throw us off course but they also contain the seeds of a better situation. Far from sending us backwards, setbacks and their accompanying discomfort are a catalyst for change. In fact, it is almost impossible for change to occur without them.

Truth

Nothing has the potential to move us forwards faster that a set-back. In fact, the power of discomfort and unhappiness to drive change is so widely observed that there is even a formula for it. Gelicher and Beckhard were a professor and an Organizational Change Consultant who spent years studying why businesses changed, or more often failed to change, even when they really needed to do so. They designed Gelicher's Formula for Change (Cady et al, 2014) to outline what needs to be in place for any change to take place.

$$A + B + D > X = C$$

For change (C) to take place three things are needed; (A) a dissatisfaction with the current situation, (B) a vision of something better and (D) an understanding of first steps to get there. Together these three things need to be greater than cost of making that change (X), whether that cost is financial, physical or emotional. Gleicher and Berkhard were analyzing organizations but this formula fits neatly with most situations, including those of Charlotte's clients. The thing to notice here is (A), dissatisfaction with the current situation. Without a significant level of things being pretty darn rubbish, change will not occur. Things being bad is literally a prerequisite for things getting better.

This doesn't mean that setbacks aren't painful, teeth gnashing, unfair, bruising, frustrating and sometimes all of these at once. It doesn't mean that they don't upset our equilibrium and set us back for a while. But we tend to see events as either good or bad, as positive or negative when in fact setbacks can be both things at the same time. Both positive and negative. Somewhere in the painful plate tectonics that overturn our plans, new paths and new possibilities emerge. We become unstuck. While things look strange and unfamiliar at first, after a while we realize that things can't be better without them being different. Nothing sets us on a new path forwards, faster than a setback.

For some people the events that trigger these changes are seismic ones like redundancy, illness and business loss. But even small discomforts can remind us that it might be time to change things up. Faris Yakob is one such person who has overcome the fear of fluidity and change, in an endeavour to shape his life in a way that brings him some degree of peace. Having done 'aggressive career laddering' after university he finally earned a place on the board of a prestigious 3000 employee-strong advertising agency in New York City. He was 30 years old, (about 20 years younger than other board members), earning a large wage, with a corner office and also deeply unhappy. Fifteen years on he now runs a boutique consultancy business with his wife Rosie, and lives a nomadic lifestyle with no fixed home country but instead traveling the world to deliver projects and speaking engagements. The many and continuing shifts and adjustments to their way of life are driven by their desire to find a good balance of physical and mental health that was absent from their New York corporate life. He talks about it like an active fine tuning, constantly being alert to what is and isn't working and regularly course correcting as needed. 'Seneca said the hardest thing to know is what you want, so we use a little guiding point to help us.

It is a piece by a children's artist called Dallas Clayton that says, "Make a list of the things you love. Make a list of the things you do every day. Compare and then adjust accordingly."' On Faris and Rosie's list is travel, solving complex problems, speaking and teaching – so they shape their work and life around this list. Initially triggered by his rejection of corporate life, they continue to course-correct as life throws up new things such as missing family and community or the travel ban during the pandemic. Rather than this being a constant grasping for something better, Faris talks about it more as an acceptance that things change and while they try and be happy with their current lot, they simultaneously try to 'hold onto things lightly' knowing that things change and they may need to let them go. (Source 10)

If letting things go and accepting discomfort still doesn't sound too appealing, then this might convince you. The more we encounter setbacks, the better we get at encountering them. Not only do they provide the catalyst for change and possibly a comedy anecdote in years to come, they also strengthen our ability to deal with things going wrong. The more we experience discomfort the more of it we can handle. This is because resilience and coping ability isn't something we are born with like good genes and curly hair, it is a muscle that we can strengthen. And the rule of making strong muscles is 'no pain no gain'. Discomfort isn't just a stimulus for growth but also for strength. The natural world offers up an analogy to illustrate how this works. When environmental researchers created the Biosphere 2 project in the USA, they were thrilled to find that the trees grew far more rapidly than those outside the biosphere dome. They were less thrilled to find that they fell over before reaching maturation. After examining the roots and bark it was discovered that the lack of wind meant the trees failed to develop 'stress wood', a key component for strong growth. Without this component the trees simply couldn't support themselves in the long run. The trees needed some stress to survive. Like trees, if we humans remain permanently in our comfort zone, we lose touch with how we manage when we go outside it. Each of us has our own set of tools for dealing with emotionally difficult or stressful situations but if we are constantly in a stress-free, warm bath then these tools get rusty. The more often we encounter situations where we are challenged and go into our stretch and even our panic zones, the more we build our confidence and resourcefulness at dealing with more of the same. For people with mild anxiety, therapists will often encourage them to take small steps into their stretch zone, to try out activities or experiences that they are a little anxious about, in order to build their confidence bit by bit at what they can deal with. Conversely, being wrapped in too much cotton wool can lead to us just requiring more layers of cotton wool as we become less and less courageous and less used to the discomfort of challenge or change. It seems at odds with a world where self-care is the name of the day, but the truth is that a little of what we don't like can also do us good.

THE TOOL

Rather than the familiar phrase 'good, better, best' this tool explores 'bad, better, best'. The aim is to help reframe our thinking around a situation being a negative setback and examine it to see what potential good stuff might emerge. This isn't about blind optimism and denying that anything has gone wrong. It is trying to see the potential for an occurrence to be good and bad at the same time. Change offers possibilities so this tool gets us to reflect backwards and forwards to see where something good can emerge from a change that at the time seems anything but.

Start with exploring some past events to get you in the groove. Think through the 'bad, better, best' of some past events that occurred and scour your mind to see what good stuff emerged from something stinky. The tables below are populated with some examples to show how this might work.

Past events

TABLE 1.1   Bad, better, best table to explore past outcomes

Bad Set back that has occured	Better One good thing that came out of it	Best One wonderful thing that came out of it
I didn't get into the university I wanted.	I met an incredible set of friends at the uni I ended up going to.	One of those friends stayed with me for life and was best man at my wedding.
I had to homeschool my children while working full time during the pandemic, which was beyond stressful.	My children loved spending so much time with each other and mum and dad during that time.	I saw more of my children over that year than I had since they were babies.

Current events

Now move on to some situations that you are currently facing that seem wholly negative right now. Try to imagine some possible good outcomes that might emerge. Even if these exact scenarios don't come to pass, it will diffuse your worry that this will be an irredeemable disaster!

TABLE 1.2   Bad, better, best table to explore possible outcomes

Bad A set back that is currently occurring	**Better** One possible good thing that might come out of it	**Best** One truly wonderful thing that might come out of it
I have got on well with all my line-managers before, but I'm really not sure about my new boss.	I might learn some first-rate people-handling skills by working with someone I don't naturally click with.	I can leave and find a job that suits me even better than this one.
My son won't study for his exams, no matter how much we try to encourage him.	We'll learn that, as his parents, we can't micromanage his life at this age.	If he fails it might be just the tough life lesson that he needs.

THE INSPIRATION

Kris Hallenga, Founder of CoppaFeel!

Kris Hallenga has achieved an incredible amount for someone in her mid-thirties. She has written a *Sunday Times* Top Ten bestselling book, been featured in documentaries and founded the breast cancer awareness charity CoppaFeel! Most significantly she is the woman who has convinced a generation of young women and men to check their breasts. When Sara speaks to her from her home in Cornwall where she also runs a coffee and cake van with her twin sister, she is warm, funny, smart and candid. So far so perfect. So what is Kris's secret? What good fortune came her way that set her on this fulfilling path?

Kris's secret is most people's nightmare. Aged 23, having had pain in her breast for some time and having been repeatedly ignored by doctors, Kris was diagnosed with incurable stage four breast cancer. Overnight her world turned on its head: 'Suddenly, there was no thought of career. There's no thought of real big, normal life decisions. There was only a lot of time at the hospital and treatments and recovery at my mum's house.'

Kris's book is called *Glittering a Turd* because alongside the decades of treatments, pain and uncertainty, cancer has led her to lead a life she had never thought possible. From visiting Downing Street to saving hundreds of young lives through CoppaFeel! While cancer is most certainly still a 'turd' for Kris, she shows beyond doubt that even the worst moments of life have the potential to unlock vast amounts of glitter.

Kris reflects that before her diagnosis that she wasn't destined to become a high-profile and dynamic campaigner. Far from it. She had just come out of a bad relationship and was traveling and teaching in China but she didn't have clear plans for what came next.

I was a bit of a drifter before that. I was hardworking, conscientious, all those things that you classically hear in your reports from school. I was very dedicated to what I was

15

putting My mind to, but I hadn't ever found anything that really, really sparked this huge enthusiasm, passion, and drive until I was diagnosed with cancer. Before that I was definitely not a campaigner. I'm very much not a problem solver, action person. I was just a person who was happy to just let other people lead, happy to be the bystander for a lot of things. So, yes, cancer was transformational in so many ways for me.

Kris's diagnosis turned her life on its head but as well as the avenues it closed down for her, it opened up others. It brought her a cause that ignited her sense of passion and injustice so strongly that she couldn't ignore it.

It came at a time when I was also looking for a purpose. I was looking for something that gave me some direction in life. So, the two collided. The charity was born out of a very strong need to educate young people, because no one else was doing that. Once you have a lot of time on your hands, you start thinking about your predicament quite a lot and I couldn't help but consider that for so long, I didn't know that I should be checking myself, I was ignoring symptoms for such a long time. Having spoken to all my friends and them not being any wiser about breast cancer themselves, I thought, 'Well, surely there needs to be something that helps people like us be more vigilant or empower us and educate us about something that actually affects so many women and men every year.'

Before Kris had even finished her first chemo treatment, she set off with a group of friends to a festival with a very loose plan to talk about the overlooked risks of breast cancer in young adults and Coppafeel! was born. It was almost non-negotiable for me, I needed to do something. It never crossed my mind that I would wait, that I'd wait to find a time, because I couldn't imagine a better time. I couldn't imagine a time where I wasn't having treatment because I was obviously diagnosed with an advanced cancer. For me, my life was treatment now, there was no end to it. So, there wasn't really a better time in my mind at the time… I smile a little bit at this young, naive girl who just really threw herself into something that she knew nothing about. I think, 'Well, respect to her. She just did it.' I think that took a lot of gumption, and I only really understand that now.'

As well as being the seismic shift that changed the course of Kris's life for better and worse, her diagnosis also serves to help her rebalance day-to-day life towards one that serves her better.

It definitely has finetuned what I want. It gives me a good navigation on, 'Does this thing make me happy? Oh, it doesn't? I'm not going to do it anymore. Do I want to do that thing that I know isn't going to give me the joy I want? No, I'm not going to do it.' And so, it definitely helps me. So, I definitely think I'm much better at saying no to things, saying yes to things. Just being aware of what my needs are, and them being non-negotiable. I don't pander to other people's needs. I pander to my own.

As well as the many things that Kris's diagnosis took away from her, it brought her many other wonderful aspects to her life. Her story goes to show that even the largest of turds can also come with a huge side serving of glitter. Does it need to take a setback as huge as Kris's to realize the benefits that can come from positive discomfort and change? Kris doesn't think so. 'This doesn't have to just come from a cancer diagnosis. It can literally just come from life.'

Conclusion

We like things to be black and white, but the truth is that lots of life events can be both bad and good at the same time. While setbacks upset our equilibrium and cause discomfort, sometimes that is exactly what is needed for positive changes to occur.

CHAPTER TWO

It's all about now

'What day is it today?' – A question asked by many. Also, a question used to assess whether someone is composmentis.

O n working with now, because there can be power in the status quo. Our temptation is to find all of our answers in the past or in the future. This chapter explores the potential of working with the now.

Myth – You should focus on what's ahead of you, or analyse what has come before.

Truth – Own the moment and the situation you're in.

Living in the now is difficult because we are forever encouraged to think about the future or conditioned to dwell on our past. Advertisements, reminders, notifications, messages, and alerts are all so often geared towards any time other than the present. A ping from your phone and your train of thought is gone. Not focusing on four things at once is seen as a sinful neglect of the multitasking skills you worked so hard to master, while enjoying a one-on-one conversation or simply taking some time for yourself is quite often written off as lazy and inefficient. Well, this chapter is about to challenge these so-called standards and show how more effort on now, and less on later or before, will help you increase your happiness, gain more control and move forwards more productively.

Myth

We grow up with an expectation that we can somehow manipulate time. We think we can influence the present by over-analysing the past or somehow change what's coming by sending telepathic waves into the ether. But most of us aren't in the movie *Bill & Ted's Excellent Adventure*. While a certain degree of retrospection and vigilance are no doubt helpful in informing our actions today, there is a danger of growing too attached to these hopes or fears and losing sight of what is staring us in the face, right now. To quote one of our favourite literary figures, Albus Dumbledore, 'It does not do to dwell on dreams and forget to live.'

A Harvard University study showed that people spend 47 per cent of their waking hours thinking about something other than what they are doing. Which equates to half of our lifetime not being engaged in what's happening right now. And, guess what, this failure to focus on the immediate world around us is making us unhappy. The study's authors, Matthew Killingsworth and Daniel Gilbert, observed: 'The ability to think about what is not happening is a cognitive achievement that comes at an emotional cost.' (Killingsworth and Gilbert, 2010). Unlike other animals, humans spend a lot of time thinking about what isn't going on around them: contemplating events that happened in the past, might happen in the future, or may never happen at all. Indeed, mind-wandering appears to be the human brain's default mode of operation. 'I've had a lot of worries in my life, most of which never happened' was reportedly said by Mark Twain but is something all of us will relate to.

This unhappiness may well be caused by the fact that our anxieties are often correlated to the uncertainties of the future, and our sadness is rooted in events of the past. As Amelia Aldao, a clinical psychologist, put it, 'by staying grounded in the here-and-now, we can lower the pull that these emotions can have on us.' (Garis, 2020).

As we'll come on to discover in this book, one of the commonalities our Rebuilders share is their relationship and appreciation of time, the present in particular, and the role they thus allow the past and future to play in their everyday lives. Contrary to popular belief, the success rate of rebuilding a business or life isn't predetermined by the severity of our catastrophe. People who have experienced truly awful events aren't less likely to rebound than people who have experienced something mildly unpleasant. In fact, you will observe that individuals with truly devasting pasts have come back in the most affirmative of ways. Perhaps because they didn't have a choice, perhaps because they have a predisposition that helps them seek the opportunities in opposition, or maybe they were lucky enough to have someone help them through it. Equally, you will no doubt know people who have had minor stumbles and can't unstick themselves from this setback, reliving it over and over again. The success of a rebuild is predicated by how much attention you pay to the here and now, and how much you lose yourself to another time zone.

Perhaps because of their relationship to the past, another characteristic our Rebuilders share is their lack of regret. Looking backwards and ruminating about events that have passed isn't part of their modus operandi. They have worked at identifying value in each of their experiences and try to leave the distractions of the past and future behind. 'What can I do now?' is their response in a stressful situation. And more importantly, 'what should I stop doing now?' to make the present a happier, more fulfilling and successful place to be.

Truth

Cutting out distractions from the past and future to focus on the now sounds so simple. But, as with all things simple, they need to be mastered first. What then are the best ways to stay grounded and see value in the here and now?

Let's get in the flow. This method emanates from positive psychology and has become a popularized expression to describe everyone from athletes to rappers at their most focused. 'Flow' is considered a mental state in which a person performing an activity is fully immersed in a feeling of energized focus, full involvement and enjoyment of the activity. Key to this state of enjoyment and productivity is the elimination of distractions, defining your goal and picking the right task that strikes a balance between your skill level and being challenging. The Harvard University study we mentioned earlier in this chapter showed that people are at their happiest (and least distracted) when making love, exercising, or engaging in conversation and at their least happy (and most distracted) when resting, working, or using a home computer. What's critical here is the focus you dedicate to the task at hand. Especially if you are trying to get through tasks you love less (as all of us must do from time to time). Giving it your undivided attention will help you get through it faster, do a better job and who knows... maybe even come to loathe it a little less!

Dr Mihaly Csikszentmihalyi, who coined the term 'flow' in the 1960s, observed:

> The goal [of finding and using your flow] can be anything from learning a language, doing great work, sports, or playing an instrument. You could even get in the flow while doing the dishes. The only factors are that the goal needs to require your fullest attention and to provide clear cues to measure your progress. Flow is important both because it makes the present instant more enjoyable, and because it builds the self-confidence that allows us to develop skills and make significant contributions to humankind. (Csikszentmihalyi, 1990).

If getting in the flow of things doesn't sound quite right for you, you might consider this next technique which has gained an exponential following over the past decade: mindfulness. Once considered a hippy dippy, incense burning pastime, it has since been discovered and transformed into a performance tool used by the US military, Google, in classrooms and by large corporations. No wonder the industry that has formed around mindfulness techniques is predicted to reach $2.08bn in 2022 (MarketData, 2017).

So what is it about mindfulness that helps us hone our perspective so effectively?

Mindfulness works by purposefully bringing one's attention to the present moment without evaluation or judgement, helping to eliminate all distraction and thought patterns that take us away from the present moment. It's an ability that every human being already possesses; it's just a matter of learning how to access it. Seven core attitudes help us access this kind of mindset:

1 **Non-judgement.** The objective is to enter a state where we become an 'impartial witness' to our own experience by developing an awareness of our habits to constantly judge ourselves and others.
2 **Patience.** This is the act of understanding that things will unfold in their own time. Even if we have to wait a little while for results. We should give ourselves permission to take the time and space necessary for mindful practices, without attaching any particular outcome to them. Just see what unfolds!
3 **A beginner's mind.** Our beliefs and what we think we know blinds us from seeing the world as it is. Mindfulness practices try to cultivate a 'beginner's mind', in which we try to see everything as if for the first time. That is to say without any preconceived expectations.

4 **Trust.** We should trust that each of us has wisdom within ourselves. Mindfulness is about learning to trust that basic wisdom. Start paying attention to your feelings and intuition and don't ignore them just because someone told you to.

5 **Non-striving.** Meditation takes a certain kind of work and energy, think of it as *non-doing*. But this is not the same as no effort. It's more about being present with intention while letting go of the outcome. This is the most difficult mindfulness attitude to embrace because almost everything we do, we do with purpose or a goal in mind. But when it comes to me meditation, goals are more effectively gained by *backing off from striving* and focusing deliberately on seeing and accepting things as they are. Acceptance thus becomes a touchstone for growth.

6 **Acceptance**. Acceptance means seeing things as they actually are right here and now. Now this does not mean that you have to like everything, or that you have to take a passive attitude and abandon your principles. It is simply having an open mind to see things as they are right now.

7 **Letting go**. Our mind has a tendency to hold on to good experiences and reject the not so good ones. Meditation practice encourages us to stop dwelling on the good and rejecting the bad and instead, when we become aware of the mind's impulses to do so, recognize them and choose not to pursue them any further. We just observe and let go, or notice, and let things be.

The evidence for its effectiveness isn't just anecdotal. Scientific evidence suggests that mindfulness can improve brain and immune health, mental health, helping to manage chronic pain and improve sleeping patterns amongst other things (Walton, 2015).

What both the flow and mindfulness can help manage is our obsessive – and slightly abusive – relationship with time travel and the distractions that this brings with it. Setting aside past or future events and possibilities can give us the space to get the best out of now, to focus on what we can control and allow us to see people and situations from a neutral and fresh perspective. Having the tools to discover contentment and opportunity in the present can help us eliminate anxiety and stress that comes with trying to control the uncontrollable and influence the impenetrable.

A masterclass in putting this process to the test is Tiger Woods. He recently shed light on his recovery process, following a car accident in early 2021 that severely injured his right leg. Woods is no stranger to a setback, or comeback, having experienced personal and professional scandals and defeats over the past decade. From affairs and a high-profile divorce, knee and back injuries, a big comeback and win at the 2019 Masters and his 2021 car incident, he has developed an upbeat and realistic view of his progress and recovery, focusing on the immediate goals and accepting the things he is unable to change. When he spoke to Golf Digest in an exclusive interview in November 2021 he said, 'I don't have to compete and play against the best players in the world to have a great life. I can still click off a tournament here or there. But as far as climbing the mountain again and getting all the way to the top, I don't think that's a realistic expectation of me.'

Having previously recovered from five back operations, Woods describes the recovery process as climbing Mount Everest. A difficult journey fraught with setbacks, a lot of hard work and not a little amount of positive mental attitude which often draws into focus the small wins and a new appreciation of what each day can bring.

'I'm just happy to be able to go out there and watch [his son] Charlie play, or go in the backyard and have an hour or two by myself with no one talking, no music, no nothing. I just hear the birds chirping. That part I've sorely missed' (Rapaport, 2021).

THE TOOL

SOAR is a simple process that helps us keep our mind and actions focused on what's immediately in front of us. This isn't to suggest that we shouldn't ever consider the past or future. These will obviously play an important role in the right time. But on the occasion that we find ourselves at a tricky impasse because we're feeling anxious, lost or out of control, this can prove a helpful process to reset our thinking and rebuild our next steps.

Set short-term goals. Set yourself goals and tasks that you can get on with straight away. For instance, preparing for a good meeting tomorrow, or what to make for dinner or which days to exercise. Setting goals that can come to fruition in a timely manner helps us regain a sense of control and progress.

One task at a time. Don't multitask yourself into a frenzy. As soon as you split your attention too many ways your mind and focus will start to wander and you will feel less fulfilled by what you are doing. This isn't about pushing work off your plate. It's about sequencing it so you can give each task your full attention and get the most out of it.

Accept what you are hearing, seeing, feeling and understand it in the context it is happening in. We spend a lot of time regretting decisions because we would make them differently today. This is because context is forgotten very quickly after an event unfolds. By accepting what was or what is, we allow ourselves the freedom to move on instead of wasting energy trying to fix or change something that has come to pass.

Respond, don't react. Pressing pause for a moment and not reacting to everything that is thrown your way will give you space to consider your next step and help you control the outcome you want to achieve. Make your actions more considered and more satisfying for yourself and others.

THE INSPIRATION

Howard Napper, well-being advocate, stress expert, meditation teacher

Howard came to be an advocate of living in the now by excessively living for the now. He grew up on Kings Road on London in the 1960s, and upon leaving school became the apprentice of a renowned fashion designer. Having landed his dream job, Howard fully immersed himself into the lifestyle of a young apprentice working in fashion: shows, parties, drugs and alcohol. While fun for a while, the stimulants that provided a good time initially, became the source of some really dark times and, over a decade later when his daughter was born, Howard decided enough was enough. His destructive habits had to stop. Initially reluctantly, he joined a friend at a yoga class. Howard notes that at the time yoga was still very much a niche pursuit, with the singing and chanting Hare Krishna as its main ambassador. Nonetheless, he joined his friend and found himself transformed, not so much by the physicality of the movements and poses, but by the meditative process. The chanting, the repetition, the breathing… Howard describes it as a profound experience that moved him and has stayed with him ever since. 'It changed my life. Actually, it saved my life in many ways. Using the body to change our relationship with thought. It's not just about flexibility and being a great form of exercise.' The idea that changing our mind and thought process starts with our body and not our head sounds counterintuitive to most of us. But therein lies the power of these practices.

Howard is now a passionate ambassador and teacher of well-being practices that help everyone regulate their physical and mental health. He draws on breathing work, meditation, yoga and other mindfulness techniques into a stress management practice he calls 'Body Based Mindfulness'. In London he has created a drop-in stress class that helps its participants focus on the three main components of Body Based Mindfulness. **Breath** (using breathing techniques to control the central nervous system), **body** (using your body to reset your mind) and **time** (time being one of the most valuable gifts we can give ourselves).

Our relationship with time and giving ourselves time is so important. When we're stressed, we make a lot of decisions based on fear because we're on high alert. We switch into survival mode. And those aren't always the best decisions to make. When we're stressed, we get caught up in the drama, the melodrama of a situation, and the stories we tell ourselves become a distorted reality. Whereas when you can cut all that out, you are left with something very different. A stillness. And peace. And it doesn't matter what is happening externally. You can tap into something that creates this experience and gets to what the essence of something is.

When tackling a problem or a bigger setback, Howard is a big advocate of stepping away. 'You can't think your way out of an issue. More meetings, more brainstorming won't solve it.' If a bunch of stressed people are sitting in a room, panicked, trying to figure something out, you probably won't get to the same answer as a bunch of relaxed and confident people who haven't lost perspective or nerve. So what should you do then?

'Sleep is one of the best way for the body to metabolize stress. Other ways include breath exercises, participating in a hobby, walking in nature, etc...,' Howards says. Anything but just relying on thinking your way out of it. He then tells the story of Elias Howe, credited with inventing the modern lockstitch sewing machine. Elias was trying to figure out how he could use the needle, which was threaded at the top, to puncture the fabric and leave the thread embedded in the fabric. Nothing he came up with was working and no matter how late he sat up trying to figure it out, with pen and paper, with models, with sketches, he couldn't think of a way to make it work. According to a family history of his mother's family, this is what happened next:

He had dreamed he was building a sewing machine for a savage king in a strange country. Just as in his actual working experience, he was perplexed about the needle's eye. He thought the king gave him 24 hours in which to complete the machine and make it sew. If not finished in that time death was to be the punishment. Howe worked and worked, and puzzled, and finally gave it up. Then he thought he was taken out to be executed. He noticed that the warriors carried spears that were pierced near the head. Instantly came the solution of the difficulty, and while the inventor was begging for time, he awoke. It was four o'clock in the morning. He jumped out of bed, ran to his workshop, and by 9, a needle with an eye at the point had been crudely modelled. After that it was easy. That is the true story of an important incident in the invention of the sewing machine. (Draper, 1900).

Who knows whether this story is true or not. But it makes a really important point. A lot can be solved by detaching yourself. Stepping away. Taking a walk. Or just sleeping on it.

This focus and ability to drown everything out is something Howard says we see in athletes who under pressure look for ways to find what they call 'the zone', or the flow, as we explored earlier on in this chapter.

I love tennis. It's such a tactical game. And you have to be so focused. If you miss a ball you have to let it go immediately. And you see some players who are still thinking about the point they missed two games ago. It completely throws them off. They can't get back into that process. Because they can't accept it. You need to focus on the process. A lot of athletes will have routines to get them into that place. They will have triggers. Footballers might touch the pitch, then cross themselves before a match or kiss a lucky medallion. Tennis players will do all kinds of things with water bottles and towels. These are routines and rituals. To induce that state of being. When they prepare for a tournament, they're not thinking about winning a match. They go through the process. One ball at a time.

And that is something we can learn from as we try to focus on the essence of a rebuild and cut out all the unhelpful and often negative noise that makes life, quite frankly, less enjoyable.

Conclusion

Maybe you're a fan of mindfulness, or have developed a ritual that gets you in the zone, or perhaps you're not too sure about either of those things. If you take one thing away from this chapter let it be that there is nothing wrong with living in, observing and enjoying today. Not multi-tasking, not forward planning, not ruminating about what could have gone better in that meeting. If you make the most of what you can do and influence right here, right now, there will be more good things to come, and much to feel good about later on.

CHAPTER THREE

Ignore the uncontrollable

Almost everything in my life that I've had to let go of has scratch marks on it. Well put, supposedly by
DAVID FOSTER WALLACE

On investing in what you can control. Knowing what you can and can't change and channelling your energy only into the things that you can affect can feel like a cop out. This chapter explores why focusing only on what you can control is a fundamental tool to rebounding from a setback.

> **Myth** – You should want to control everything.
> **Truth** – Don't waste your energy on the stuff you can't change.

Myth

Building a wall of control around us helps us feel safe and structured in some way. It wraps us in stability, certainty and a degree of control. But if we don't have control, we feel anxious, beat ourselves up and become worry warts. Because our instinct tells us that the more we worry, the more we can somehow affect the outcome. Of cancer. Of a pay rise. Of winning a new piece of business. Of recognition. Of your children's development or your partner's fidelity.

Generally, our energy equation goes something like this: the more time you spend on something = the greater your ability to influence the outcome. Therefore, the more you worry, the more control you gain over the situation, right? Well, actually, not so much. We tend to conflate the worrying bit with the impact bit.

The Covid-19 pandemic – the great leveller that has created many shared experiences – has taught us all a first-hand lesson in control. There are certain things you can do to improve your chances of not getting sick, but ultimately there are so many factors beyond our control that there is no guarantee for anything.

What each of us could control during the pandemic was: wearing a mask, getting our vaccinations and boosters, using hand sanitizer (often!) and keeping a safe distance, preferably outdoors.

What was entirely out of our control: people who saw themselves above those basic requirements, transmissibility of strands, public policy, and your personal predisposition or precondition to getting ill.

So there is a lot you can do to minimize risks, but there are no guarantees. Worrying about the 'no guarantee' bit won't change the outcome. But it will drain your energy, challenge your mental health and lock you into a downward spiral of anxiety and stress.

None of this will come as a surprise. In a rational moment, or following some distance to a situation, most of us will have come to a similar conclusion. But why do we keep on doing it?

Our need for control, or our need to perceive that we are in control (even though we're not) isn't all bad. In his book *If You're So Smart, Why Aren't You Happy?* Raj Raghunathan argues that having control helps us believe that we can shape outcomes and events to our liking (Raghunathan, 2016a). That is, the more in control we feel, the more efficacious we feel about achieving the outcomes we desire, and this sense of competence boosts well-being. Studies have even shown that those with a higher need for control generally set loftier goals and also tend to achieve more (Artino, 2012).

But it can also go too far. When you seek to exert control over uncertain situations that are impenetrable to our influence and try to control the outcomes, you set yourself up for failure and disappointment. This drive to control can make you, and those around you, miserable. The well-known motivational psychologist David McClelland calls this 'power stress,' which is the tendency to get angry and frustrated when others, or the environment around you, don't behave the way you want them to (Raghunathan, 2016b).

And when we're overly controlling of others, our decision-making suffers, because we drive away those who disagree with us and thus surround ourselves with only those who don't mind being controlled: the 'yea-sayers'. Ultimately, we make our best decisions when we are exposed to a diverse set of views and inputs and if you seek to exert too much control in these situations, the independently minded will tell us where to stick it.

Truth

So there is a lot we cannot and should not control. Equally, we don't just want to drift and see where life takes us. What then is the happy medium between taking charge and letting go?

The clue might lie in the well-known Serenity Prayer, reportedly written by American theologian Reinhold Niebuhr in 1933 (Wygal, 1940).

> God, grant me the serenity to accept the things I cannot change,
> courage to change the things I can,
> and wisdom to know the difference.

Let's start with 'spotting the difference'.

The things you can't control: external factors; other people.

What you can control: yourself, your actions, your reactions.

Ask yourself: Is this a problem I can solve? Or do I need to change how I feel about the problem?

You can give your employees the tools they need to succeed, but you can't force them to be productive. You can make sure you're driving responsibly, but you can't control what other people will do on the road.

When you strike a healthy balance of control, you'll see that you can choose your own attitude and behaviour, but you can't control external factors. When you stop worrying about those, you'll have more time and energy to devote to the things you do have control over. And this can be key to reaching your greatest potential, a new perspective and a rebuild.

Someone who has learnt this lesson time and time again is the eminent Mandy Sanghera, international human rights activist and advocate for victims and survivors of honour-based violence and cultural abuse such as female genital mutilation, forced marriages, faith-based abuse and witchcraft. Mandy has dedicated much of her life to helping women and children flee abusive and dangerous relationships, working with NGOs, governments and private individuals to extract them safely and help them rebuild their lives in new communities and countries. In this process, certainty is one thing Mandy has learnt to live without. 'It's important to be realistic,' she says. 'You want to help everyone, but you can't. You have to manage expectations with clients and be honest and authentic. And let go of the things if they are out of your control.'

In Mandy's line of work, lives are literally at stake. Pressure and emotions run high. Since the 2021 withdrawal of the US and UK troops from Afghanistan, Mandy has received many desperate emails and calls. Women, men, families hoping to escape the Taliban rule. When I spoke to Mandy, she was off-grid, laying low in an unidentified location in England, having received multiple death threats from the Taliban who were displeased with her efforts to rescue outspoken women. 'Fear is only inside your head,' Mandy said confidently. 'But when you're dealing with these intense situations, it's so important self-care starts with you.' Sleep, meditation and an hour long walk in the countryside help Mandy stay focused and grounded.

Extracting each person from Afghanistan was a huge undertaking. Coordinating private planes, paperwork and getting the green light from government departments in host countries, then getting individuals to the airport in Kabul. So much can go wrong. So many aspects of a rescue mission are completely out of Mandy's and her clients' control. It's always a huge team effort. Mandy has learnt to become pragmatic about the process. 'You can't take setbacks personally. Use them as fuel. Learn to accept your own limitations and use your network for support.' Mandy has also learnt to compartmentalize her challenges. She said she pictures her to-do list and her worries as an inbox. Never downloading everything at once. The things she has no control over and can't do anything about at that particular point in time she mentally files under 'pending'. They are there, not forgotten, but not consuming her mental energy when there is nothing she can do about it. If she doesn't think she can help someone, she is upfront about it. She takes one person at a time and recognizes that even one person saved is a win. Mandy is not one to voluntarily offer up how successful she's been. 'I work for the cause, not the applause,' she says. So it's nice to take this opportunity to recognize that throughout her career, Mandy has helped save 300 children from marriage, 80 women from domestic violence, 13 victims of witchcraft, and helped at least 87 Afghans escape the Taliban.

While in Mandy's line of work, uncertainty can be disconcerting, in other instances uncertainty is actually desirable. Take, for example, our desire to avoid knowing who got booted off the latest episode of UK's *Strictly Come Dancing*, or America's *Dancing with the Stars*? It's also why most of us, if given the chance, wouldn't want to know how long we will be on this earth for. That type of uncertainty is intensely engaging, liberating and motivating to keep going.

Consider this piece of research, referenced by Todd Kashdan, a leading expert on the psychology of well-being, curiosity, mental flexibility, and social relationships, in his book *Curious?* (Kashdan, 2013). Researchers told participants they would receive a free dollar. One group was asked to imagine that they would learn why they received the dollar soon after getting it, while the other set was asked to imagine that they wouldn't learn the reason. Both were then asked to indicate how happy they would feel upon receiving the dollar. The first set, those who expected to know the reason for receiving the free dollar, thought they would feel happier than the second. In fact, the opposite happened. Those who didn't learn the reason for the free dollar were happier. Concluding on his findings, Kashdan suggested that 'what we think brings us pleasure', in this case certainty and control, 'is often the exact opposite of what does.'

THE TOOL

If you are still feeling uncertain about your relationship with control, and uneasy about the prospect of flourishing without it, here are a few technics to help you acclimatize and realise the full potential of life a little less certain.

FIGURE 3.1   Considerations for navigating control in uncertain situations

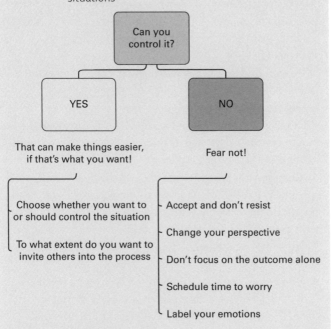

If you CAN control a situation

You are most likely to be in your comfort zone because you can affect the outcome, or at least you feel like you can.

That said, just because you can control a situation doesn't mean you should. You might decide that, for whatever reason, it's better for you not to interfere with the action, or it might be the wrong time for you to step into a situation and assume control. But these are deliberate decisions you can actively take.

If you CANNOT control a situation

Don't panic. Hopefully, by now, you will be able to identify the merits of accepting what you cannot impact or change. That doesn't mean it will always be easy or that you won't be resisting your gut instinct to gain control! Here are a few ways in which you can sooth that anxiety and start to manage it.

Accept and don't resist. Accepting that unpredictability is a fact of life can help you let go of any unhealthy or unrealistic desires to try and bend the universe to your will. It's nothing personal. It's just a fact of life. We've found the turn of phrase 'it is what it is' quite liberating to say out loud, multiple times, in times like these.

Change your perspective. Being in the heat of the moment can make any situation seem more challenging and frustrating than when you give it a little space. If you don't have the benefit of time, try adopting a different perspective. What would someone standing on the outside say about your situation? How might they observe what you find stressful or challenging to control? Or how might you feel about it in three years' time? What is the long-term impact of not being able to control this particular situation? These techniques will give you a sense of perspective.

Don't focus on the outcome alone. Helen Weng, a clinical psychologist and neuroscientist at the University of California San Francisco suggests that we're better off focusing on the intention of our actions, rather than insisting on a certain outcome (Purbasari Horton, 2019). Focusing on intentions and aligning these with our values, such as honesty, creativity or loyalty, will be able to influence what is happening, without expecting a certain outcome to materialize. Anyone who has had a birthing plan will know it almost never happens how you planned it to, no matter the amount of preparation!

Schedule time to worry. Said no one ever. But it's actually a really useful psychological trick. The trick involves scheduling time to worry. It sounds odd and the opposite of what you feel like doing, but studies have shown that it actually works (McGowan et al, 2013). Set aside some meaningfully short time to worry about things that are causing anxiety (15-20min should do it). Block it out in your Outlook or Filofax. Or set your Apple Watch to remind you. Make it a regular and consistent occurrence. That way you can dedicate 100% of your attention to playing every mutation of every scenario through and free up the rest of your day to get on with other things.

Label your emotions. This is another counterintuitive but effective method. If you're experiencing anxiety or frustration because you're not able to control a situation, or because you fear uncertainty, give that emotion a name. Research has shown that mere verbal labelling of negative emotions can help people recover a sense of control (Lieberman et al, 2011). This is called 'affect labelling'. (Not to be confused with over-thinking and dwelling on negative emotions which is called 'ruminating' and tends to only compound your negativity and anxiety. For example, replaying an argument over and over again in your head and focusing on all the bits of the argument that really bothered you without being able to move on)

THE INSPIRATION

Sarah Libbey, Founder and Director of The Longhouse London, a marketing and advertising headhunting firm, mother of three, breast cancer survivor

Sarah is a great example of someone who, seven years ago, learnt a lesson or two on being happier by detaching from an outcome. Sarah is a single the mother of three and has run her own successful business for nearly two decades. Sarah would definitely have told you she likes to be in control of everything, anticipating any bumps in the road and planning her work and life in order to minimize disruptions. Then she was diagnosed with breast cancer. She hadn't experienced any symptoms or noticed anything wrong. On an off chance, to complete a health assessment she was referred for a mammogram – just to tick the box. Sarah put on an incredibly brave front to everyone around her. Making light of side effects and other changes that were thrown her way. But one thing that was harder to stomach than anything else was the lack of certainty doctors could give her around her recovery. Sure, statistics were offered up, but nobody could look her in the eye and tell her that they were 100% certain she would be ok. She felt out of control, and no amount of googling could put her mind at rest.

Realizing there was precious little she could do about this conundrum, apart from continue her treatment and support her recovery as best as possible, she had an epiphany. She decided to change the way she approached the problem, rather than try to solve it. She made peace with the things she couldn't control. Instead, she focused her attention on the aspects of her situation she did have an influence over. For example, her own outlook and attitude. Taking each day as it came, without obsessing over the next month or three. Being ok with not knowing her destination, and not letting that stop her from taking one step at a time and enjoying what was immediately in front of her and up for grabs.

Thankfully, she fully recovered. Her life is back to its hectic and chaotic state of normal, but she has clung tightly onto her new relationship with uncertainty and applied it to running her business as well. In fact, when the Covid-19 pandemic hit, she felt much more at ease than many of her friends when it came to questions around how long we would be in lockdown for, or when business would pick up again. Sarah took each day as it came and didn't let her hopes or fears for the future derail her ability to be fully appreciative of the day ahead. Rebuilding her health and her outlook have yielded a few other tips she wanted to share, transferrable to a business environment as well as your personal life:

- **You don't need to be totally broken before you reboot yourself.** Being ill has taught Sarah that there are so many changes you can make before life or business goes off piste and often we wait until it's really bad or almost too late to make a change. You can reboot at any time. Don't wait for rock bottom.

- **You don't have to know where you are heading** or what the solution is before you decide to make a change. Too often we won't improve or address a situation if we can't say or promise where it's going to end up. Especially in business. Trust that each step can bring progress, and that progress is rarely a linear and efficient process. Control what you can control.

- **Managing the people around you** on your journey is important. This can often come at the expense of sparing people's feelings; but learning how to **ask for help,** letting people in, and giving others the opportunity to show their true selves is important.

Conclusion

Uncertainty is often experienced as one of life's great curve balls. If only we could always be sure and know the outcome. Or even better, be in total control of life around us. Hopefully this chapter has demonstrated how uncertainty needn't hold you back, and, in some cases, how it can even promote joy, liberation and fuel to embrace the first steps of a rebuild.

CHAPTER FOUR

Stop peeking into the past

*'I just want to go over what happened one more time,'
we say to ourselves as we rake over the remains of
the latest mishap.*

On how to stop looking back and start looking forwards. Who hasn't indulged by wallowing in hindsight? Or analysed the mistakes of each misstep? This chapter focuses on the merits of freeing yourself from what's come before and looking ahead to what could be next.

Myth – If we examine past mistakes hard enough we won't make them again.

Truth – We must stop looking backwards if we want to move forwards.

'Regrets, I've had a few,' crooned Frank Sinatra back in the sixties, articulating a sentiment that many can chime with. Who among us hasn't given themselves whiplash, craning back over our shoulders to dissect what just went wrong? All the while feeling the pull of regret and remorse that accompanies these retrospective reviews of our mistakes. And why not? Hindsight is supposed to give us 20/20 vision so if we can rake over what went wrong for long enough, surely we will learn what not to do next time around?

Myth

This natural urge to examine past mistakes has some sense in it. If we suffer a set back and things don't go quite as we had hoped, then there might be lessons to be learned. In Chapter 9 we explore what we can learn from failure but the short version is that we can learn a lot, but not everything. We might gain some experience and learn some pitfalls to avoid but, and it's a big but, it doesn't guarantee that we won't make another mistake. It doesn't even guarantee we won't make exactly the same mistake for a second time! After all, Elizabeth Taylor got married eight times including twice to the same man (Holborn, 2018). In short, looking back has some benefits but those benefits are finite. Eventually we need to stop looking backwards in order to move forwards.

Psychotherapy offers us insight into why. Imagine a scene in your life that didn't go well. A bad break up, a disastrous meeting, a job loss, a worrying health diagnosis. You mentally revisit the scene over and over in your mind, exploring and inquiring into what led to that moment, what could you have done differently and you would change it if you could. Looking back is part of processing what has happened but too much looking back can start to hold us back and the psychotherapy term for it is 'rumination'. Susan Kay Nolen-Hoeksema, American Professor of Psychology at Yale University, defined rumination as 'the focused attention on the symptoms of one's distress, and on its possible causes and consequences, as opposed to its solutions' (Nolen-Hoeksema, 1991). In layman's terms this means too much time spent thinking about what went wrong and not enough time spent planning for things to go right.

One problem with constantly looking back is that it can lead to us feeling more miserable and worried. As we constantly relive what happened, it keeps the distress fresh in our mind. In extreme cases leading to anxiety and depression (Nolen-Hoeksema et al, 2008). The other challenge with too much ruminating is that it doesn't actually help change our situation. Far from helping us avoid future set backs, it keeps us stuck in the problem rather than working towards solutions. If the whole point of looking backwards is to help us avoid issues in the future, then at some point our energy is better spent on planning for that future.

Nancy Reyes, CEO of top creative company, TBWA\Chiat\Day NY has a wonderful expression to capture the lure of ruminating on issues. Nancy's journey with TBWA New York began in 2016 when she joined as part of a leadership team tasked with bringing the agency back up to full strength after several tough years. As a smart and empathetic leader, she spent a lot of time talking to staff to try and get to the bottom of the issues that the company was facing and to listen to challenges being raised. 'It's important to diagnose and analyse and give some airtime to grievances and negative issues in any kind of company.' But after a few months she realized that the problem examination had the potential to be never ending. If the agency was going to move forward, then it needed to start looking at what lay ahead, not what had already happened. 'At some point you need to stop admiring the problem and spend more time addressing it and moving forwards. Because the truth is that if you spend so much time on the negative side, you'll never fix it.'

'Admiring the problem' is such a perfect expression for the urge that we all feel to go back and keep on replaying and re-examining what went wrong and what might have been. So if you, your team or your organization find yourself spending too much time with what went wrong, Nancy's words are a great reminder that if we spend less time admiring the problem and more time admiring the solution, we are more likely to get out of the hole we find ourselves in.

Truth

To build a picture of how to move forwards after a setback, we decided to explore one of the toughest losses that any of us face – bereavement – and the process of grieving that helps us process loss and begin to look ahead to our life once more. It might sound a little leftfield or dramatic to compare other life events to grieving processes but bear with us. All losses can be viewed as processes of grief, even if the scale of their impact is never as great as a bereavement.

> Grief doesn't just belong to death. That's really important. We can grieve other things. We can grieve friendships, we can grieve people that we could have been, job opportunities. Covid-19 has been a huge learning in terms of all the things that we can grieve and how we deal with that grief. It's not like we spend our whole lives not experiencing grief and then when someone dies, it hits us. There are lots of practices along the way. And if we can find a way to better deal with our grief, I think when it hits us really hard, we'll be better prepared.

These are the words of Anna Lyons who is an end-of-life doula supporting people living with life-limiting illness and their family, and friends. Her aim is to help people live as good a life as possible right up until the end. Together with progressive funeral director Louise Winter, whose mission is to get people to rethink funerals, their platform 'Life, Death. Whatever' explores all aspects of this much-avoided topic. So passionate are they about generating wider discussion and understanding that they wrote a book called *We All Know How This Ends* which explores lessons about life and living from working with death and dying (Lyons and Winter, 2021).

Lots of literature refers to the 'five stages of grief': denial, anger, bargaining, depression and acceptance (Kubler-Ross, 2014). Anna notes that these were originally written about dying, not about the grieving process.

People can give themselves a really hard time if they're not going through those five stages. Because, grief is quite chaotic and different for everyone. But the key thing is to find a way to go through it, to learn to live with it, and whatever that takes.

More helpful is William Worden's 'four tasks of mourning' which lays out the tasks that he feels must be done for 'the process of mourning to be completed' and 'equilibrium to be re-established' (Worden, 2003). These can happen in any order, and he accepts that people may need to revisit them over time. As well as relating more traditionally to bereavement, they provide a really helpful way to think about rebuilding after all manner of set backs or losses.

The first task is to accept the reality of the loss

Death equates to loss. Birth is the start of something, death is the end of something, and very often the end of something that we're not ready for… that we don't want to end. The grief is not just about the loss of the person. It's the loss of the life you had imagined, it's the loss of the future that you had planned. We have to somehow try to forge a new future. Oftentimes, that's not the future that you want. So, it can feel even more difficult, because we have ideas about where we're going in our life, we make choices, and we choose people to go along with us. And then all of a sudden, they're not there… that life that you had planned isn't going to happen.

As Anna says, this same sense of loss for the future aims and dreams, is keenly felt after many of life's set backs. The relationship ended, we didn't get the job we dreamed of, the house move we were hoping for fell through. We had a path planned out and a dream or an ambition that we were excited about and suddenly that is taken away and replaced by sadness, frustration and a feeling of a rug pulled out from under our feet. Acceptance means acknowledging that the path we had planned won't unfurl as we had hoped. In time there will be a comeback, but it will be along a different route than the one we had planned.

The second task is to experience the pain of the loss

No one wants to hear that it's going to be painful, but it is. The more we can lean into the pain, frustration or anger, the less power it will have on us over time. In the case of bereavement, Louise Winter is a strong advocate for how vital good funerals are as a way of people coming together and sharing the emotions of loss and sadness. 'A good funeral at its heart is a way of bringing people together to share emotions, to support each other and acknowledge that life will never be the same again.'

Elsewhere, there are as many ways of experiencing the pain of loss as there are people. Some people scream, some go quiet and Adele writes songs that make anyone who hears them cry their eyes along with her. Tom Ilube is one of the UK's foremost technology entrepreneurs and educators and he has developed his own technique for processing failure or loss in business. 'I have a good technique. When I fall flat on my face, I cry like a baby. I will cry with pain, agony and fury and then I will bounce back. Then I get up, brush the dirt off my shoulder and move on to the next challenge.' (Ilube, 2011). Whether you favour a big cry or a platinum-selling album, the key is to let yourself feel the pain, frustration and anger in order to move past it.

When Anna speaks about the power of sharing our pain and feelings, she is talking specifically about death and dying, but the sentiment rings true for so many of life's losses.

> I think we hold a lot. When we don't express how we feel about something, we hold that, it comes out, it leaks out. I think just knowing that it's okay to express how we're feeling, what we're feeling, what's going on, even if those things feel really ugly to say out loud, having the permission to do it, knowing that those thoughts and feelings will be held by somebody, that they won't be judged by someone, I think that in itself is releasing and healing.

The third task is to adjust to an environment with the 'deceased' missing

Your new reality is just that, new. Life isn't quite the same now your friend has moved abroad, your business has shuttered or your youngest has left home. Something is missing that has caused your world to shift and now there will be some adjustments to be made. Some of these will be very practical such as looking for a new job or dealing with the paperwork of a divorce. Others will be emotional. Who do we rely on now that the landscape of our relationships has changed? How do we think about our identity now the business that we founded has closed?

Together, these three tasks create an ending which has to occur and be recognized before we can move on to the next thing. No new story can begin until the previous one has come to its end. This applies just as much for the professional realm as it does for the personal one. Dean Shepard, Chair in Strategic Entrepreneurship, Indiana University, has written at length about how loss in business manifests as a form of grief and how important it is to allow time to work through it. He has shown that negative emotional responses from business loss are so damaging that they 'interfere with the ability to learn from the events surrounding that loss'. He has shown that without a 'process of grief recovery' people can't even process learnings that they might salvage from such a difficult event (Shepard, 2003).

When businesses face set backs, how many of them create time and space for people to process loss? To mourn the loss of the big vision they were chasing or the colleagues and plans that are no longer a part of their day-to-day? Perhaps it is a failure of business during turnarounds to rush too quickly past what has occurred and to brush setbacks under the carpet. Far better to let teams process the loss before trying to re-engage them in whatever plans need their energy and imagination next.

Worden's final task is to reinvest in the new reality

This is where we stop craning back over our shoulders and start to look forwards. One of the most powerful ways to reinvest in a new reality is to create a rich and exciting vision of what you want to happen next. What is the dream for this new path you find yourself on? As Anna says about bereavement: 'Life will never be the same, that life that you had planned isn't going to happen. But that doesn't mean that there can't be a life, a different life that is full of wonder.'

Engaging our imagination and creativity to envision what this rebuild could look like is a powerful tool in helping us let go of the past. This may take the form of writing down what you would like to happen next in your life; where you want to be next year, exactly what your new job will entail, what your new house will look like, what an ideal day would be. You might be someone who likes to draw or use images to create a picture or perhaps just talk it through in detail with a friend. The method doesn't matter, what is important is that you engage your imagination in reinventing your new reality. *A* new reality so thought through that you can feel it, smell it and see it so clearly that you are drawn towards making it happen.

Please don't worry if this all sounds a little like Instagram advice telling you to go and make some vision boards. There is strong science behind the role that internal creativity and vision play in getting us to move in a new direction. No, you can't just sit on a yoga mat and manifest a million dollars. But yes, if you are trying to move on from a difficult set back then projecting your mind forwards will help kick start momentum and get you unstuck. For many years sports people have used visions of winning and success to keep them motivated. Therapists encourage patients to envision good outcomes to aid those stuck ruminating over or intellectualizing a difficult period in their lives. The use of positive mental imagery and future visions plays a key role in Cognitive Behavioural Therapy, where the focus is on shaping desired future actions and reactions rather than unpicking what has happened in the past.

THE TOOL

If you are struggling to let go of what has happened, then revisit Worden's first three tasks of grief and ask yourself if you need more time to really accept and experience the pain of your loss. Do you need to take more time to process and accept an ending?

If you feel ready to start to envision a new future then try the tool below. These questions use a solutions-focused approach to take your mind forwards and mentally create a picture of what comes next.

Select two questions below which capture your imagination and relate most to your situation. Most of these can be tailored to work or personal life as you wish. Set aside some quiet and reflective time to spend on each one creating a really detailed answer. Write, draw, record voice notes, share with a friend. Whatever works.

By doing this exercise you will start to see insights, ideas and inspiration emerge that can be used to build a practical pathway towards the solutions that will form your come-back.

Solution-focused visions

What is your 'future perfect'? If money and resources were no option, what would be the dream?

What would you like to have more of in your life or work? How could you achieve this?

Describe the ideal day, five years from now. What are you doing? Who is with you? Where are you? What is taking up your time? What are you looking forward to?

What would life look like if you woke up tomorrow and your goal had been accomplished? How would you feel? What would be happening?

What is your goal? How will you know that your goal has been reached? How will others know your goal has been reached?

THE INSPIRATION

Hope Patterson, Founder of A Bunch of Deckheads

Hope Patterson was going to the NBA to play basketball. In his mind this was never in question. It was the dream that he poured years of blood, sweat and practice into. Having been introduced to basketball by a youth worker, he was so determined to be the best he could that he was often criticized for over training by trekking across London from Tottenham and Walthamstow to Wimbledon on Saturdays to attend multiple basketball runs. After growing up in Tottenham with an alcoholic, abusive, absent father, basketball was his chance to get out from under his older siblings. 'It was my way of having my own identity and being known for that.' The game even shaped his values and lifestyle and he laughingly says it kept him away from both alcohol and girls until he was in his late twenties.

Today in his forties, Hope is about as relaxed and smiling as a person can be. He laughs easily, shares his story readily and gives off a warm and confident energy. So when he explained to Sara that this NBA dream never happened, she was interested in knowing why – and also how on earth he has maintained such a positive and optimistic outlook on life. How did he avoid a life of dwelling on what could have, should have, might have been?

Aged twenty, Hope was playing for Goldsmiths College and The University Of London when he was diagnosed with scoliosis, or curvature of the spine. Told he would never play basketball again, he went into hospital to have a metal rod inserted into his spine. After nine months of wearing a back brace doctors agreed that because of his outstanding physical shape going into the operation, he could pick up the sport again safely. He had triumphed over adversity, or so it seemed. Within six weeks of removing his brace, Hope was attending The Atlantic Camp Basketball in New Jersey where he was offered a number of scholarships to play at Caldwell College, University Of Pittsburgh, DeSales University and Cairn University.

After a tough couple of years, finally his dream was coming true. Then Hope turned the scholarship down. Financially he just couldn't make it work.

> They were only part-scholarships so they would pay for my fees but not my living expenses. I just couldn't support myself financially and I would have needed to be trying to work on top of studying and I knew it wouldn't work. I had seen the quality of the other players and having just had the year out with my back injury I knew that I would need to be devoting every spare minute to training and playing which was what a lot of other players would be doing.

The combination of his operation plus his financial circumstances meant that he had to let this dream pass by. While his friends went off to play at Princeton and George Washington State, Hope returned to the UK where he played for the Brixton Topcats, one of the UK's top National League teams. He always thought the chance would come around again but aged 28 he decided it wasn't going to happen and quit the game.

The end of this dream took time to process and Hope felt lost for a couple of years. He started a new career in the city which paid well, allowing him to buy property, watches and cars but didn't give him the 'joy, happiness and validation' that basketball had. But fast forward a few years and Hope found a new dream to anchor his life. He was DJing full time and loving it. He had started playing as a hobby but got better and better, landing residencies in London and Oslo. After a few years he had so much work he started his own business, A Bunch of Deckheads, representing over 80 DJs, working with brands like Hugo Boss, Rockstar Energy Drinks, Twitter and ASOS and opening for Stormzy at SnowBoxx Ski Festival in France.

What was it that allowed him to let go of one closely held dream to eventually find another while harbouring no anger at the cards fate dealt? On reflection, it is clear that Hope invests so much in bringing his dreams to reality that he knows there is nothing to regret when they don't pan out. He didn't just dream big with basketball, he dreamed enormous. 'I had an unrelenting desire to realize how good I could be, and I had a really clear vision and a goal in mind. I wanted to be the best shooter in world, but I also wanted to be a beautiful basketball player. It was about being the best that I could be because there is no point otherwise.' When it didn't come to pass he knew there was nothing more that he could have done. 'At the time I felt with the resources and information available to me, then at the time, it just made sense. Given how late I had started playing and the progress that I had made was a testament to how hard I had worked at it. So I felt like I pretty much left it all out there. In my mind there wasn't any more that I could have done.'

He could have stayed working in the city, as many others do, but during those tough, lost years he still strove to uncover a new dream. While basketball hadn't worked out it had gifted him the knowledge of what it feels like to do something that you love. 'It's having that thing where you want to do it. And it's almost an obsession. It is an obsession. And if what you're doing doesn't afford you that, then you have to ask yourself what you're doing.' He calls this feeling an 'infinite pursuit…where inspiration defies logic, where you're trying to realize an ideal, an objective, where you try to discover how good you can be and you enjoy the process.' When Hope started playing out as a DJ, he found another possible infinite pursuit and he reinvested in a whole new reality.

> I just keep posing the question to myself 'what's possible and can I do it?' And then that pulls me onwards… because you've only got one life and you want to try and make it as rewarding as possible. And yes it's going to come with challenges. And yes, it's not going to be fair, and you will be beset with tragedy, bad luck and misfortune but where you've got the capacity to make it as rewarding as you can, as enriching as you can. You grab that and you own that.

Hope reflects on what his DJ career has brought him, saying 'it astounds me to this day that a passion has afforded me so many opportunities.' He is amazed and grateful that opportunities have lined up with his passion. Listening to him, Sara couldn't help but think that it is precisely because he is so passionate that the amazing opportunities have come.

Conclusion

When setbacks happen they mean the loss of something in our lives. Our plans, our dreams, our hopes for how we thought things might turn out. We need to allow ourselves to feel and accept that loss before we can reinvest our energy in what comes next. But when we feel ready, we should jump into that new reality with both feet and to dream as big and glorious as we have ever dared to do.

PART TWO

How to tackle comebacks

CHAPTER FIVE

Whose fault is it anyway?

'Everyone needs to own up to their part in this mess before we can start to clean it up,' *we think to ourselves after as the dust settles on disaster.*

On **responsibility.** We need to step out of the blame game if we want to move forwards. Embracing our own role in every situation is the secret to feeling in control of what comes next.

Myth – Things can only be fixed when we know who broke them.

Truth – The only responsibility we should look to is our own.

Success has many fathers, but failure is a bastard. This all too familiar phrase hints at how hugely subjective allocating responsibility can be. After things go awry, it is a very natural instinct to want to explore where blame and fault might lie. After all, if we are going to rebuild then everyone needs to step up, own their part and learn from it, including ourselves. Unfortunately, the reality of allocating responsibility is slippery and elusive. So let's dig deeper into the role responsibility can have in a rebuild and whether it is a critical step or a wild goose chase.

Myth

'Responsibility' and its evil twin 'blame' are very much in the eye of the beholder. We have all met people who take everything to heart and when things hit the skids they immediately look at the log in their own eye. Much hand-wringing and introspection may ensue which isn't always wholly productive. Equally, we have all met people covered in Teflon who let nothing be laid at their door and who no fault or blame ever sticks to.

We only need to read the news on any given day to see cases where judges and lawyers battle it out over this exact topic, to realize how tricky allocating responsibility can be. Who did what to who, and who is responsible for their actions and the ensuing calamitous outcomes is the cornerstone of every prosecution and defence. Who was the villain and who was the victim? It really isn't always clear cut.

Take the high-profile fraud case of Elizabeth Holmes, disgraced Silicon Valley CEO of the now defunct medical testing company Theranos. In 2021 she was charged with fraud after allegedly misleading investors, including Henry Kissinger and Rupert Murdoch, to raise $700m. Theranos had claimed for many years to have developed revolutionary blood testing technology, but the company (valued at $9 billion) collapsed when scientists and regulators discovered the technology didn't work. On the face of it, who is at fault seems pretty obvious. Assistant US Attorney Robert Leach says 'This is a case about fraud, about lying and cheating to get money... by making misstatements to investors and patients, Elizabeth Holmes became a billionaire' (McCluskey, 2021). However, her defence team points the finger at a range of other causes and contexts such as the pressure to succeed in Silicon Valley and psychological abuse by her then-partner. They claim she 'is actually a living, breathing human being who did her very best each and every day' and simply failed – which is not a crime. So if she tried her best, can she really be to blame for the ensuing disaster? (Godoy, 2021). In January 2022, jurors found Holmes guilty of conspiracy to commit fraud and wire fraud and was awaiting sentencing. She continued to deny the charges which carry a maximum prison term of up to 80 years in total (BBC, 2022).

Even in far more mundane, day-to-day events there are multiple and opposing views about who is to blame. When an East London resident was facing parking fines for a series of driving offences, rather than pay up he decided to turn the tables on the council who had issued then. Claiming the fines caused him 'emotional distress' he took Newham Council to court and was awarded £20,000 by a judge, £5,000 damages for each ticket he was issued (Smith, 2009).

These examples highlight the subjectivity involved in any attempt to assign responsibility. In the cases of both Elizabeth Homes and the parking tickets there are clear benefits to those on each side of the blame game. All parties have things to gain or to lose that skew and obscure any objective view of who should really be at fault. We find this crops up all the time in our Rebuilders research. Where people think responsibility sits often has little to do with where it actually sits and more to with the different agendas of people involved. Be it a failed business or a failed marriage, looking to untangle the motivations and agendas is often a thankless endeavour. One that might explain why lawyers make so much money.

But it's not just people's personal motivations and agendas that muddy the waters. There is lots of research to indicate that the results of our actions are hugely dependent on context. While we may like to believe that we are the masters of our destiny, there is a fair dollop of happenstance and circumstance thrown into the pot which makes it even tricker to really untangle the roles people play in situations. One area where this has been proven to be true is the high-flying world of leadership. While powerful leaders may wish to believe that their actions and ideas make the difference between success and failure, a professor at Harvard has shown that even senior leaders have little or no real impact on the organizations that they lead. In what is almost certainly an ego blow to many 'big cheeses' out there, Gautam Mukunda explores a large amount of social science evidence to ask whether 'individual leaders are truly responsible for the end result, or do they just happen to be there, for better or worse?' (Mukunda, 2012). He concludes that there is a web of factors that govern the results of most leaders, all of which are far less sexy than just being a unique and talented genius! Factors include the external context and environment which limits a leader's ability and discretion to act. The internal politics and organizational dynamics which leaders must attend to. Plus the fact that most leaders have similar experience and are selected using the exact same selection process means the pool of potential senior recruits are hugely homogenized. A recruitment wind tunnel that helps to ensure the wholly unqualified or incompetent leaders don't end up at the steering wheel, but also ensures that many of the top candidates might be interchangeable in their impact. 'Take General Electric. What if GE's board had picked someone other than Jack Welch as CEO? Would the company have performed the same? Most likely, GE would have chosen someone quite similar to Welch had he not accepted the job', Mukunda says. Because of this, Mukunda calls Welch a leader of 'low individual impact. It's likely that another candidate chosen by GE management would have performed nearly or as well as he did.' (Girard, 2012).

This highlights the challenge that often the environment we find ourselves in plays a huge role in how things turn out for us making our context possibly more responsible for outcomes than our own actions. These circumstances beyond our control are acutely present when we think about issues of privilege and lack of privilege. The notion that anyone can get anywhere with a bit of hard work fails to recognize the huge systemic bias that works against many of the less dominant groups in society.

Even without these systemic biases working against many in society, there are infinite examples that prove to us that a huge web of factors other than our own actions and talents affect our outcomes in life.

Consider this ingenious example from a young and aspiring writer called Chuck Ross. Ross had written a mystery novel but despite his high hopes, the manuscript was repeatedly rejected by publishers. He was convinced that many of the publishers had barely even glanced at the book before turning it down, so he devised a cunning plan to prove that there was much more influencing the publishers decisions than the merits of the writing. To prove this, he submitted the manuscript of a bestselling novel by award-winning writer Jerzy Kosinski, to multiple publishers under a different title and author name. The National Book Award winner was rejected by every publisher. Without Kosinski's name on the cover the content wasn't deemed good enough to print (Green, 2013).

It is clear that trying to unpick who is responsible for what is fraught with bear traps. Personal agendas skew our notion of where accountability lies plus context, environment and even societal biases shape how things may turn out. So where does this leave Rebuilders? Do we just abandon the idea of trying to understand who was accountable for what in our endeavours to move forwards? How do we then understand our own part in what has happened? Do we throw personal responsibility to the wind or does that sound a little irresponsible? And how do we not see ourselves as victims of circumstances if nothing is really within our control?

Truth

The sports field is a helpful place to look when exploring these questions. Whether a team wins or loses is very clear but in team sports it is trickier to figure out which individual contributed what. We spoke to Sir Clive Woodward, England's 2003 Rugby World Cup Winning Head Coach, to understand how he approaches responsibility and accountability with his players and he revealed a concept he uses called 'window/mirror'.

> What window means is, when you win the big game, you start any debriefs with 'window'. In other words, you look through the window and you credit everybody else and never talk about yourself. Look through the window, you can say the other players are great, the coaches are great, my parents are great, everyone is great. You don't talk about yourself, you talk about other people and what went well. When you lose the big game you 'mirror'. The only person who has got to take responsibility for that is the person in the mirror. When we lose, don't blame me because I'm blaming myself and I'm looking in the mirror and saying 'this is my fault. I'm the head coach who lost the game'. But I need the team also looking thinking 'Okay, what did I really do?' Rather than asking if it's this guy's fault, or that guys fault. The only person to blame is the person in the mirror. What

you're really asking for is for people to take real personal responsibility.

Sir Clive strongly cautions against blaming other people because those are influences outside ourselves that we cannot change.

He also stresses that this isn't just about apportioning blame or praise after the fact. This approach is about encouraging everyone on a team to take personal account-ability and control for whatever they can to ensure in advance that a win happens. This means speaking up in advance of matches if they feel things aren't right.

> During the week in the build-up to a game... if you don't think we are right you say so. I'm not precious about this. And I'll be saying 'Is everyone OK? Are we good to go?' If you don't think we are good to go and you don't stand up and say then we will fall out big time. I want people to say 'No we're not good to go. What about this? We haven't done this.' By the time it is Saturday I want everyone in the room knowing we have been absolutely spotless in terms of how we have prepared. Don't come complaining on Monday morning after the fact saying we should have done this and that.

What Sir Clive Woodward nails here is that the only responsibility we can usefully look to is our own. The person in the mirror. There may be many factors at play in how things turn out but rather than seeing ourselves as victims and blaming others, there is great power in focus-ing on the one thing we can control, ourselves and our own efforts and actions. Then win or lose we know we have done all we can. This active choice to focus only on our own actions and contributions also supplies a great feeling of strength and wrestles some control back from the universe. When times are turbulent and events are rocky, feeling in control is a super power. It also helps us to let go of things through the 'window'. To stop internalizing responsibility for people and things outside of our control and to let those areas of fruitless worry go.

While this approach is still alive and kicking with Clive and many others today, it is a way of viewing life that has stood the test of time. As far back as the 3rd century BC the Stoic philosophers believed that it is not the events in life that matter, but our judgments over and reactions to these events. No doubt this helped them cope with the frequent wars, unrest and back-stabbing that were rife back then. Sartre too held onto this view as the central idea of existentialism. He believed that man is fully responsible for his nature and choices so while we cannot choose our circumstances, we can choose how we act and react to them. It is no coincidence that these beliefs arose at a time of great civil unrest while Sartre lived through the second world war and occupation of France and himself was a prisoner of war in 1940.

This way of thinking can be hugely empowering when life gives us lemons. Despite our best efforts, sometimes circumstances beyond our control set us back. Remembering that even when events are out of our control, we still have the ability to choose how we respond, is hugely powerful. This is why we hear about people time and again, in the toughest of situations, digging deep to choose how they react. One of the most powerful and beautifully told stories of this type is the book *Man's Search for Meaning* by former prisoner of war Victor E. Frankl. Frankl was a highly respected psychiatrist taken to Auschwitz in 1944. After many years of imprisonment and the loss of his family he survived against all odds. In these most horrific of circumstances Victor found meaning in choosing how he responded and he later wrote that this saved his life. 'Everything can be taken from a man but one thing: the last of the human freedoms – to choose one's attitude in any given set of circumstances, to choose one's own way.' He believed that even in the most challenging of circumstances we still have power and control. 'Between stimulus and response there is a space. In that space is our power to choose our response. In our response lies our growth and our freedom.' (Frankl, 1959).

THE ACTION/REACTION TOOL

Ever wanted to fire off an angry email or text saying in no uncertain terms who messed up that meeting? Ever wanted to look to the sky and yell 'why me?!' after another carefully laid plan goes off the rails? If the answer is yes then you are in good company because anyone who claims never to have pointed the finger of blame elsewhere is probably lying. This tool is designed to help us take a beat to digest what has happened and then plan what we, not anyone else, would like to do about it. Between the event and our reaction to the event, we have a choice. Exercising this choice is what gives the freedom and control for what comes next.

FIGURE 5.1 Action/reaction tool to plan a considered response to events

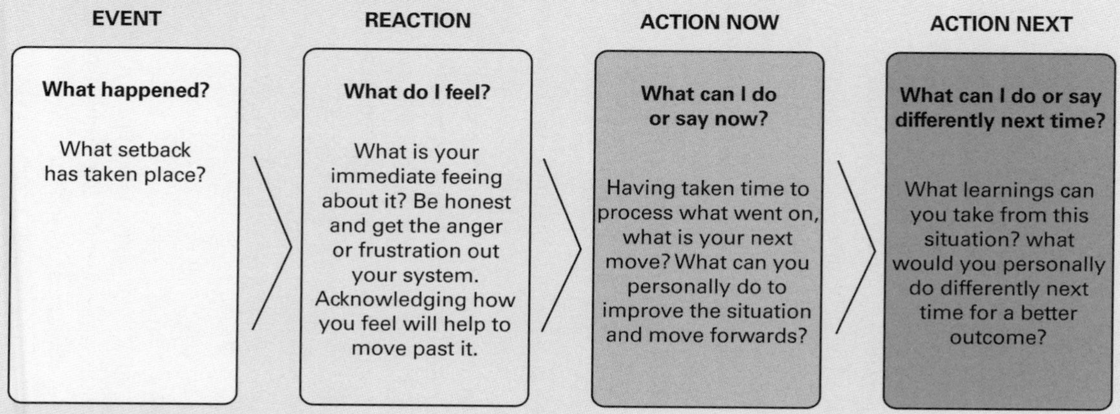

EVENT

What happened?

What setback has taken place?

REACTION

What do I feel?

What is your immediate feeing about it? Be honest and get the anger or frustration out your system. Acknowledging how you feel will help to move past it.

ACTION NOW

What can I do or say now?

Having taken time to process what went on, what is your next move? What can you personally do to improve the situation and move forwards?

ACTION NEXT

What can I do or say differently next time?

What learnings can you take from this situation? what would you personally do differently next time for a better outcome?

THE INSPIRATION

Jason Gonsalves, Global Brand Director, *The Face*

Jason Gonsalves is the Global Brand Director of iconic, British style magazine *The Face*. After a stellar career in the creative world of advertising and media he took a radical leap to leave his corporate life to successfully relaunch the much loved but then defunct magazine in 2019. A brave and bold thinker who admits to loving uncertainty, he reflected on how an early life event taught him the need to embrace personal responsibility. A period of rebuilding and reflection after getting divorced aged 31 awakened him to the power of accepting full control for his actions and outcomes and helped him roll with what life has thrown his way in the subsequent years.

Having now been very happily married for several years, Jason reflected back on what the ending of his first marriage taught him.

I think the biggest thing that it did for me in a profound way was make me stop and be really clear about who I am. Stop and examine my own faults, strengths and things that make me me. I emerged from that time by being really clear about what was my responsibility, what things were really brilliant and what things needed to change. I emerged being really honest with myself about who I am, warts and all. These realizations have been a massive part of the things that kept me sane, strong, and probably enabled me to do a lot of things since. Being really self-aware in a very unswerving way has really been a huge part of why I have enjoyed the next 20 years.

At the time, I was angry, I was upset, I felt like I'd failed. I can distinctly remember the two paths. One was feeling it was all the other person's fault and that I was just going to go out and party and have a really good time and forget about them. The other was that I'm going to think about taking some responsibility and look inside myself. To do things like a proper personal inquiry and spending time to think and reflect, and I chose that path. I'm incredibly glad I did because it's been a massive source of the strength and contentment I felt today. Of course, there are issues beyond our control. But forget all the excuses and ask yourself 'How have I been operating? What makes me tick. And what do I learn about myself?' And I think if you can be really honest and clear about that, then everything else becomes easier.

It also brings it down into things which are within your control. When there's so much that isn't within our control, try to be aware of yourself and how you show up. What is your responsibility? What can you control? This wrestles a bit of control back from the universe.

I remember going on a course with a former job and I listened to my peers talk about work and their careers and all of them were annoyed because they felt the opportunities weren't being given to them. And I remember thinking to myself, I'm never going to do that now. If I take responsibility for everything to do with myself, then I'm going to feel like I've got no excuses. This is all in my control. And I think from that day on, I did. And it's so useful sometimes in your own head to wrestle back control from the universe. It is empowering to take responsibility. It takes control and agency away from you if you believe you're downstream of other events. The more you take responsibility for everything in your life, the more liberating is.

Conclusion

Dissecting set backs to apportion blame and responsibility is a road to nowhere. No amount of analysis and finger pointing will ever untangle the complex truth of how events come to pass as they do. It is far more fruitful to look in the mirror and focus on the part that we played. Because once we take responsibility for choosing our actions and reactions, we stop being the victims in everyone else's story and start being the authors of our own.

CHAPTER SIX

The glass is neither half-empty nor half-full

'I'm sick of being told to think positively, because it hasn't worked out well so far,' think many of us at some point in time.

On optimism. We have grown up being told that by adopting a positive mindset, everything will be ok. This chapter talks about the different ingredients you should add to your positive thinking to set yourself up for progress.

> **Myth** – Positive thinking is the key to success.
> **Truth** - Learn to balance realism and optimism.

'Don't worry, it might never happen.' An annoying phrase at the best of times. Even more infuriating once 'it' has happened and you find yourself picking up the pieces of something that has gone awry. So, what mindset should be embraced to make a success of a rebuild? Optimism or pessimism? Glass half-full or glass half-empty? Or veering wildly between the two depending on the time of day and the amount of caffeine drunk?

Myth

The vital role that having the right mindset plays in making a success of things is written about at length. Google search currently offers over 13 million results for mindset coaches! The trouble is that much of the advice out there seems confusing and contradictory. Too much positivity is labelled naïve and unrealistic but too much negativity is also frowned upon. So where on earth does that leave us?

'Think happy', 'Good vibes only', 'Train your mind to see the good is everything'. We are surrounded by magazine articles and Instagram posts brightly espousing that positive thinking is the solution to whatever we are facing. That we must embrace our PMA – positive mental attitude and that 'positivity always wins... always'.

This pervasive focus on positive thinking as the key to happy living is a relatively modern concept, popularized in the late nineties by the then President of the American Psychological Association. Incoming President Martin Seligman was inspired to reorientate psychology away from its focus on treating poor mental health and curing mental illness and towards 'making the lives of all people more fulfilling and productive' in a new movement that he named 'positive psychology' (Seligman, 1998). Seligman believed that focusing on the positive events and influences in life, like happiness, gratitude and compassion, could help people to flourish and live their best lives. Positively psychology has exploded in popularity since then but has met with criticism along the way. Some claim it has been commodified and cheapened by a booming wellness industry (Coyne, 2015). While others claim it ignores the very real issues like poverty, racism and other systemic biases and traumas that hold people back (Cabanas and Illouz, 2019). 'Positive psychology gives the impression you can be well and happy just by thinking the right thoughts. It encourages a culture of blaming the victim,' criticizes clinical health psychologist and former Seligman colleague Jim Coyne (Coyne, 2019).

Whatever the truth, we can be relatively sure that a rainbow-patterned notebook admonishing us to 'look on the bright side' probably isn't giving us the full picture. The reductive idea that optimism alone can help us to overcome tough times is certainly overly simplistic and research has proven that too much optimism can in fact be a hindrance.

In 2015, a team of researchers from the University of Utah tested the notion that optimism pays off and they came to the wonderfully phrased conclusion that 'people may be overly optimistic about just how much optimism can do' adding that 'there are lots of instances in which people think optimism will be helpful, but that belief is often misplaced' (Tenney et al, 2015). While optimistic people did try harder and work longer at the tasks researchers gave them (such as trying to find Wally in *Where's Wally?*) it didn't improve their outcomes. In fact, optimism was not only unhelpful but sometimes it was counterproductive. For example, spurred on by their positive mindset, the optimistic test subjects wasted more time and effort looking for Wally but were no more likely to find him! Many other studies have also shown the limiting effect of overly positive thinking. One study looked at women trying to lose weight and discovered that the more positive they felt about the outcome of their diets, the fewer pounds they ended up losing (Oettingen and Wadden, 1991).

Too much optimism is sometimes called Pollyanna Syndrome, after the 1913 American novel of the same name where a girl called Pollyanna maintains an impossibly cheerful disposition throughout the bleakest of circumstance. Psychologists and psychiatrists warn against the danger of following in Pollyanna's rose-tinted foot steps by being 'an excessively or blindly optimistic person' because it can reduce people's ability to deal with the trials and tribulations that exist is everyone's lives (Latecki, 2017).

So what about being a pessimist? The opposite to being a Pollyanna is to become an Eeyore, Winnie the Pooh's permanently miserable pal. The common phrase 'hope is not a strategy' even warns us that positive thinking isn't going to get us to where we need to be.

If life has served you lemons, then it might seem sensible to aim low so you won't be disappointed. Some people opt to become a 'pragmatic pessimist', who fears the worst so they can be prepared when they are let down. After all, if you think that disaster is lurking around every corner then you won't be surprised when it finally turns up. But holding on to a pessimistic outlook has its price.

Sara experienced this first-hand. Growing up in an unstable and abusive environment led her to always expect the worst.

> The children's character Chicken Licken has nothing on me. I am permanently braced for the sky to cave in and pretty good at coping with disaster when it comes along. The issue is that living this way is exhausting. Always expecting and fearing the worst takes the shine off every day and can leave me pretty shattered.

This type of thinking can arise in people who have been through very traumatic events or who experience high levels of anxiety and other mental health disorders like OCD. Extreme thinking of this kind is called 'catastrophizing' where negative thought patterns can spin out of control to imagine the worst possible outcome. However, this pattern of thinking can itself be destructive because unnecessary and persistent worry can lead to heightened anxiety and depression.

Most rebuilders hopefully won't find themselves in a full-blown catastrophizing mindset but the principles still apply, although in a more moderate form. Expecting and worrying about a bad outcome is a large drain on emotional energy and limits our ability to think creatively about what's next. Both vital resources needed to begin a journey of rebuilding.

This limiting effect on creativity and problem-solving abilities is one we will all be familiar with in the workplace. When a team sits down to think their way out of a knotty problem, nothing kills the energy like the person who likes to repeat 'we tried that before and it didn't work' after every new solution proposed. At work we call these people 'energy dementors' because of their ability to suck any positive vibes out of a room with a stream of negative comments. The team are left feeling down-hearted, any belief in finding a new solution dissolves and progress grinds to halt.

As well as simply being 'a bit of a vibe killer' there is some science behind why this type of negative and worried thinking stalls progress and kills creativity. Neuroscience research has shown that the brain cannot be fearful and creative at the same time so feeling anxious limits our ability to think of a fresh path out of a predicament (Missimer, 2020).

Truth

Learn to balance realism and optimism

The solution to this mindset conundrum comes from a Vietnamese prisoner of war camp. Not a traditional topic in chapters about positivity but bear with us. What it demonstrates is that neither pure positivity nor pessimism holds the key.

General Stockdale was an American general held as a prisoner of war in the infamous 'Hanoi Hilton' for eight years before making it out. He wrote a book about his experiences and has been interviewed often about how he managed to survive in such tough circumstances and with no certainty he would ever make it home (Stockdale, 1995).

'I never lost faith in the end of the story. I never doubted not only that I would get out, but also that I would prevail in the end and turn the experience into the defining event of my life, which, in retrospect, I would not trade.'

When he was asked in an interview who didn't make it, he said it was the optimists.

> Oh, they were the ones who said, 'We're going to be out by Christmas.' And Christmas would come, and Christmas would go. Then they'd say, "We're going to be out by Easter." And Easter would come, and Easter would go. And then Thanksgiving, and then it would be Christmas again. And they died of a broken heart.

The key he revealed was to combine optimism with raw realism. 'This is a very important lesson. You must never confuse faith that you will prevail in the end – which you can never afford to lose – with the discipline to confront the most brutal facts of your current reality, whatever they might be.'

This mindset has gone on to be called 'The Stockdale Paradox'. It is neither glass half-full or glass half-empty. It is both. It is having a powerful optimism that everything is going to be OK, plus the bravery to take on board the reality of your current situation, so you can tackle whatever is there.

Kris Hallenga is a powerful modern example of this mindset in action. Founder of cancer awareness charity CoppaFeel!, Kris was diagnosed with stage four cancer out of the blue in her early twenties. We shared more of her fascinating story in Chapter 1. Kris lives a rich life both personally and professionally, having achieved more by her early thirties than many of us do in a lifetime. And she does so against the backdrop of incurable cancer.

Kris is full of energy and positivity. While cancer has made her cautious of long-term planning, it has spurred her to do more of the things in life that bring her joy. Rather than languishing after her diagnosis, during her first round of chemotherapy she started CoppaFeel! which has grown to be the third most-recognised cancer charity in the UK. Along the way she has got a cat, moved to Cornwall, run a coffee and cake van with her beloved twin sister, talked in front of thousands and won a Pride of Britain Award. She says 'I want to be remembered for doing epic stuff, not having breast cancer at 23.' (Price, 2021).

Yet Kris is by no means burying her head in the sand. While always optimistic about her treatment options she is also a realist when it comes to the path in front of her.

> When I'm facing yet another new hurdle [in treatment], I try to consider the fact that I've been at a tricky moment before and I got through it. And here I am and I'm doing okay. Therefore, there's no reason to think that I can't be okay again. I guess in those moments feel fairly certain that I will be okay again. But I think that the amount of certainty starts to dwindle bit the more treatment options that I try. The more the drugs in the cabinet run out. There are treatments available at the start and you try those. And then, one will stop working, so you try another. That's been my life for 12 years. But at some stage, those options do run out.
>
> But what I also do is allow myself to feel all the feelings that I'm feeling and to wallow. I think I'm allowed to, and plus I don't want to be naive to what is going on with me. I don't want to be unrealistic because I think I am a bit of a realist. I don't live in some fantasy world where I believe that I'll live till I'm 90. I live in a life that I believe is finite…I think that helps me come to terms with the fact that there's work to be done in rebalancing how I'm feeling about end of life.

Kris recently started a course to become a certified 'death doula' – someone who provides one-on-one end of life care. She knows she won't practically be able to perform this role for herself but the course is helping her to face some difficult topics head-on about her own mortality.

> The course is making me confront a lot of stuff that a lot of people are very scared of. I would say that there's been moments in my life where I've been really scared to think of these things too. But in confronting them, I'm dealing with them, and then it's done, and then I can put it to bed and move on. That's how I've been accepting, coping. That is my coping mechanism, confronting something.

Kris says she is 'making friends with my own mortality' and there are few more powerful examples of embracing the realism of life than confronting the inevitability of its end.

THE TOOL

This balancing of optimism and realism is something that everyone can do. It helps keep us positive but still grounded and relieves any worries about having mixed feelings about our current situation. This 'root and branch' tool is designed to help you to focus in on those mixed feelings and explore both sides of any given situation. Simply use the questions as a guide to explore your situation and as a reference point. The roots reflect the reality of your situation. Tree roots may get down and dirty in the mud, but they are a necessary foundation and the anchor for any tree to grow.

The branches explore the most optimistic outlook. They reach up towards the light and they are where new growth and new life are going to come from.

FIGURE 6.1 Root/branch tool to balance optimism and realism

BRANCH QUESTIONS TO INSPIRE OPTIMISM

What is the outcome that I am most hopeful of?

How would that outcome affect my situation now?

What three things could I do to make that outcome a reality?

What one thing should I stop doing to make that outcome a reality?

ROOT QUESTIONS TO ENSURE REALISM

What is the most challenging outcome that could occur?

How would that outcome affect my situation now?

What three things could I do to prepare against that outcome?

What one thing should I stop doing to avoid making that outcome a reality?

A powerful example of this in action in work would be pitching at TBWA to retain a piece of business. When TBWA/Neboko in Amsterdam were competing to retain a large piece of retail business, the team explored and planned for every eventuality. A win would mean a futher few years of partnership with one of their largest and most creative clients. A loss would be a blow for the agency financially and emotionally. The agency did everything they could to ensure a positive outcome. They kept focused on what the winning solution would be and poured all their energy into weeks of tough pitching. They kept the team motivated by the prospect of winning not the fear of losing. They took every practical step they could to ensure they had the best resources and brains on the pitch and left no stone unturned. At the same time they were hugely realistic about how competitive the pitch was and never once took it for granted that the business would stay with them. A loss would mean the agency would need to change size and shape and these decisions also needed careful plannng. The CEO needed to think through every eventual outcome before he would received the result. He considered in detail how to deliver both good and bad news and how to implement any neccesary changes in the least disruptive way. As a diligent business leader he knew that all eventualities had to be planned in great detail so if they lost the business he could minimize the impact on his team. They planned for the best and the worst case scenarios until they received the wonderful news that they had indeed won.

INSPIRATION

Nancy Reyes, CEO, TBWA\Chiat\Day, New York

Nancy Reyes is a frank and fearless businesswoman who is CEO of one of New York's foremost advertising agencies, TBWA\Chiat\ Day New York. But it wasn't always this way. When Nancy took the helm six years ago. This once-celebrated agency, had gone through a fallow period and, alongside her team, Nancy was tasked with turning the business around. True to her direct and unflinching nature, Nancy didn't shy away from a frank analysis of what had gone wrong in the past in order to address and solve the issues. Nancy's approach of taking a hard look at the problems did bear fruit, as the agency tackled some thorny issues and saw some positive momentum. But after a year of this approach Nancy had a revelation. Too much looking back was stopping them moving forwards.

While there was positive momentum, the agency was still plagued by a little bit of its most recent history and what it had gone through. And I found that I spent quite a bit of time just really understanding what was going on at the agency, what troubled the agency, where were the problem areas? And there was one very astute person. It was a junior strategist, and I took him out to lunch and I said, 'Hey, what do you think I should focus on? What do you think I could do better at the company?' And he gave me one of the best pieces of advice I have ever received.

He said to me, 'Can you start to focus and put more of your energy on the people who have the same values as you do and who believe that the agency can move forward, versus the people who don't believe that? Because you will grow faster, we will grow faster, the company will move faster if you double down on the positive versus spend all the time on the negative.'

It's really about spending less time admiring the problem and more time addressing it and moving forward. I think that's the rub, that's where we can go wrong with it because the truth is, that if you spend so much time on the negative side, you'll never fix it. You've got to find the pieces of positivity that exist within an organization. The people who are ready to jump on the train today, if you double down there and spend more time there, chances are we attract more people who feel the same way and collectively make more headway than if spent all our time on the negative side. That's the biggest lesson I learned. And I think once that energy went there the progress moved even faster.

Conclusion

Setbacks might dent our rosy outlook on the world but we shouldn't let them dim our optimism completely. Far better to have a healthy mix of optimism and realism. This way we can keep our chins up while still being prepared to face for the bumps in the road that come our way. It turns out that the glass is both half-full and half-empty. But more importantly, it is refillable.

CHAPTER SEVEN

Don't wait to know it all

One doesn't discover new lands without consenting to lose sight of the shore for a very long time.   GIDE, 1927

On not knowing. All paths in life are fraught with blind spots, no matter how much we plan. This chapter explores how to confidently move forward when you don't know it all, and why getting lost might turn out to be for the better.

Myth – Don't set out on a journey without knowing precisely where you are headed.
Truth – Curiosity will get you further than knowledge.

Myth

If you only have enough information to give you a 40 per cent chance of being right then don't take action. But if you wait till you have enough facts to be 100 per cent sure, then you have left it too late. So said the late Colin Powell, Four Star General and the only African American to serve on the US Joint Chiefs of Staff (Powell, 2012). This is advice from a man who made some pretty mighty decisions with life or death consequences, so if he says we shouldn't wait to know it all then we should be inclined to believe him. He was so adamant about this as a guiding principle in both the military and in business, that he created the 40/70 formula which stated that if you have enough information to give you between 40–70 per cent chance of success, then take the decision. The point he regularly made was that waiting until you know everything can increase the risks rather than reduce them. For Powell this often meant taking decisions about military action where lives could be at risk before knowing with certainty whether his decision was the right one, because waiting longer would be too late to intervene.

While most of us aren't dealing with matters of national security, the tendency to want to wait until we know it all will be familiar to many of us. The idea that if we know more we will make better decisions is very beguiling one. Particularly if we are rebuilding after a previous outcome that was less than ideal. One more bit of research, one more conversation, one more set of facts checked then success will be guaranteed. Tempting but not true.

Colin Powell draws attention to the fact that it simply takes too long to know everything. But there is also another issue at play. Even if time was no object, it is probably impossible to ever feel that we know enough. As anyone who has ever used the internet will be aware, there is simply too much information out there and, even more confusingly, most of it is contradictory. Even if we were able to ingest the whole of Google, the information may well be redundant by the time we act on it, because the world today changes at such a pace.

As humans we are currently living in a VUCA climate. The term, first coined back in 1987, stands for volatility, uncertainty, complexity and ambiguity. Four words which send a chill down the spine of those looking for some sort of order and security in life. For everyone trying to navigate the Covid-19 pandemic in 2020 and beyond, the notion of huge global disruptions coming out of nowhere, will feel all too real. Many individuals, families and businesses now find themselves embarking on rebuilds because of an event so unprecedented that the news media almost wore out the word unprecedented.

So how can we navigate an unpredictable world where we may simply never know with confidence where we stand or what lies ahead? The first step is to let go of the idea of 'knowing enough' and just be comfortable with the idea that feeling a bit lost is not just inevitable but actually a good thing.

The messy middle

Most rebuilders are looking for a new path forward. A different job, a new relationship, a happier mindset. This means evolving, changing and undergoing a transition from where they were to where they will be next. The thing about transitions is that they need to get a bit messy for change to occur. To move from one state to another, there will be a bit in the middle where we feel a bit lost. And that's OK.

The godfather of making sense of transitions is William Bridges, an organizational consultant who spent his life studying transitions and helping others navigate them. When his first wife died, he too found himself undergoing a painful period of loss and flux which he wrote about. His book *Transitions: Making Sense of Life's Changes* serves as a guide to the professional, personal and emotional transitions that arise out of change and crisis. He says that change is the external event that shifts things in our lives, often precipitating a rebuild. The transition is the important, often gradual process, that happens inside us as we navigate and emerge from change. He helpfully creates a simple map to understand transitions. First an ending, then an in-between phase he called the 'neutral zone', then a new beginning (Bridges, 1995).

We explored 'endings' in Chapter Four. An external, VUCA event causes us to feel something has come to an end. A new boss, a pandemic, the final straw in a relationship. We generally feel a lot of unpleasant emotions, we may be demotivated, or angry or in shock. After such an ending we might expect a new beginning to emerge straight away. But Bridges and other experts in change note that there is a vital period which occurs first, the 'neutral zone' or rather ominous sounding 'fertile void'. This is the most uncomfortable stage, but it is also where the gold happens. This is the stage of feeling lost, frustrated, thinking 'argh why isn't this all sorted already'. It is the stage where we may feel like nothing is happening apart from the gnashing of our teeth and a desperate urge to pass through and out the other side. But this phase is vital to lay the foundations for a new beginning and successful rebuild. This uncomfortable, in-between stage is where transformation takes place. We shed old identities and try on new ones. Where we can explore new paths, new ideas and new ways forward. We are 'between trapezes' which is a terrifying but exhilarating place to be. And very necessary if we are to find a new trapeze to grasp.

This period of not knowing is called different things but widely recognized as being the key to successful transitions. Anthropologists call it the 'liminal zone', an in-between state where we are neither one thing nor another (Turner, 1967). Brené Brown calls it the 'messy middle' and stresses that going through the messy middle is not just unavoidable, but is actually integral to the process of change. 'The middle is messy but it's also where the magic happens, all the tension that creates goodness and learning.' (Brown, 2015).

The urge to rush through this zone and out of the other side, to relative certainty, is a powerful one. We will all be able to recall occasions where sufficient time hasn't been spent in this messy middle. Businesses rush through change programmes, often forgetting that there needs to be a period for their people to mentally transition, not simply leap from one thing to another overnight. Similarly, as individuals, we are keen to get going and onto the next thing without always allowing ourselves the space to go through the necessary adjustments. We start a job or a new relationship when we don't quite feel ready. We make big decisions in the wake of a loss or traumatic life event which can mean setting off on a path that later we regret. But when we give ourselves the time, a new beginning will come and when it does we know it is the right one and we will be perfectly ready for it.

So we can forgive ourselves for not knowing exactly what route we are taking on the journey of our come back, or even where we might end up. We can stop worrying that we don't know enough to make it a success and instead we should get comfortable with being uncomfortable. We should try to let go of the map and in doing so see what new and exciting paths and destinations might emerge. As Deepak Chopra is reported to have said, 'In the process of letting go you will lose many things, but you will find yourself.'

Truth

While the military and the economists might not be huge fans of ambiguity and complexity there is one group that we can learn from, who have long appreciated the value of not knowing. Artists have recognized that for anything truly new or creative to occur, there has to be a period letting go and unlearning.

David Bowie made an entire career out of feeling lost. He loved to unlearn what he knew before and this fueled his many reinventions. He would often shut something down at the height of its success just to see what emerged next. Bowie killed off Ziggy Stardust at the height of his powers, to explore soul and funk, then just as abruptly dropped that after that smash hit *Diamond Dogs* tour, to re-emerge as the Thin White Duke. For this master of reinvention, feeling unclear was key to the process of evolving. He claimed to handle his career in a constant state of not knowing what to do and actively prescribed getting out of your depth.

> If you feel safe in the area that you are working in then you're not working in the right area. Always go a little further into the water than you feel you are capable of being. Go a little bit out of your depth and when you don't feel like your feet aren't quite touching the bottom then you are just about in the right place to do something exciting. (Apted, 1997).

Bowie was not alone in finding gold in the messy middle. Grayson Perry also uses confusion as a way of breaking through to new ideas.

> I think I'm addicted to periods of doubt and low confidence. I think you should worry if you don't have them because then you're not trying hard enough. If you're sure that everything you're going to do is going to be good, then what's the point? I kind of see it as a sign that I'm teetering on the edge of something new. (Saner, 2021).

If Bowie and Perry aren't enough to inspire you then try returning to childhood favourite *Alice in Wonderland*. Lewis Carroll created an entire world that was one enormous 'messy middle', through the rabbit hole. Almost no one, including the reader, has a clue what is going on. Everything Alice thinks she knows about identity and reality is challenged, albeit aided by some slightly dodgy looking potions, until Alice forgets her identity entirely. When the Caterpillar asks her who she is, she replies that she knew when she got up this morning but has changed several times since then and no longer has a clue.

It isn't just flights of imagination that benefit from getting lost for a time. Scientific and technological discoveries have long benefited from the experimental approach. Setting out unsure of what will be found but with an open mind and a notebook and pen. The discovery of penicillin in 1928 that changed the course of modern medicine, was a wonderful accident. Dr Alexander Fleming was actually trying to find a cure for influenza when he noticed a strange mould growing on a petri dish after a two-week holiday. Arguably the most productive holiday in history (Markel, 2013).

What unites all these pioneers and allows them to make discoveries isn't their knowledge but their curiosity. A willingness and an excitement to think that they don't know it all and that there might be something even more exciting around the next corner if they keep an open mind. This mindset is also available to us mere mortals who haven't won the Turner Prize or chatted to a hookah-smoking caterpillar sitting on a giant mushroom.

When we began interviews for The Rebuilders podcast it was the first few weeks of the Covid-19 pandemic in the UK. It was a hugely volatile time and it was impossible for businesses and households to see what was coming round the next corner. While everyone we spoke to was feeling untethered and anxious, there were some people who stood out as tempering that anxiety with curiosity. This curiosity allowed them to feel a little less uncomfortable with the huge disruption going on and supersede worry with an interest in what might come next.

One of these people was Jason Gonsalves, the Chief Brand Officer of *The Face* magazine. Jason is a naturally curious and creative person who, through choice and necessity, has navigated several successful transitions in his life. His current role sees him at the heart of the modern British cultural landscape which continually reforms and reshapes itself. From black Westerns to the music industry's approach to climate change, Jason and *The Face* team are there to give voice to this ever-shifting cultural landscape. When Sara interviewed him, she was struck by how lightly he held onto his pre-COVID plans and how willing he was to accept the change being forced upon society, his family and his business.

I think the world right now is exhausting if you're trying to hold onto the plans that you made last year. I think it's a really good opportunity to say to yourself 'all bets are off'. It's a moment to look at things and imagine that you have a blank sheet of paper. Undoubtedly, we are going to see some really interesting, clever, amazing ideas emerge that make us see the world in a different way. I think the great tragedy would be if we returned to normality. I think the real opportunity for all of us in our individual businesses and as a society as a whole is to think of what's happened in 2020 as a 'break in series' and to actually think about what happens now given everything that's happened. What do we think the world should be like? What do we think our businesses should be like? How do we operate in a way that enriches life rather than reduces it? I think that's an exciting challenge for all of us who are running businesses and influencing the culture. Imagine that absolutely everything is up for grabs. If you wanted to, you could change your premises, you could reshape your businesses, you could completely pivot. You've got more license now to create change than we've ever had before. If your business had to be relaunched right now from

scratch with none of the legacy, what would it look like?
Because you've got the opportunity to do that.

Only weeks into Covid-19 disruption in the UK, Jason was the first person Sara had encountered who, in the depths of home-schooling his two young children and trying to keep the magazine afloat, was already starting to look ahead and wonder with some excitement what a 'new normal' could look like. The clue to what enabled him to do this is his love of unanswered questions. He wasn't immune to worry and disruption, but his curiosity allowed him to adapt to disruption with speed.

> I love uncertainty. I actually think I thrive on it to some extent. I think it's because my attitude is always to be led by the questions, not the answers. And so for me, what I get excited about is not having a plan, but having some good questions. That's how I tend to approach things and enables me to talk and bob and weave and respond in different ways. But I get much more excited by really, really good questions than I do by thinking I've got an answer.

The Buddhists have a term for this open and questioning mindset. They call it a 'beginner's mind'.

> If your mind is empty... a space may be required here depending on the source. it is open to everything. In the beginner's mind there are many possibilities, but in the expert's mind there are few. (Suzuki, 1970).

Having a beginner's mind means being open to the possibility of not knowing which in turn opens us up to the possibility of learning new things. Like Grayson Perry, it means forgetting about proving yourself right and knowing all the answers and instead exploring what new ideas and solutions might be out there. The good news is that having a curious, beginner's mind is something we can all cultivate with a little practice.

THE TOOL

'Curious'

Small children are constantly curious – as anyone knows who has been asked 'why' a thousand times by a toddler. They are always learning something new and are very comfortable with not knowing, exploring, and experimenting, but we begin to lose this curiosity as we get older. We prefer knowing the answer to asking the questions, and the desire to prove ourselves right crowds out learning. This tool aims to help regain some of that childish curiosity which will help us explore the unknown and increase our ability to learn.

Even better news is that while we are exercising curiosity, our brain chemistry and limbic system make it very hard to be anxious at the same time (Missimer, 2020). So if you are feeling a little unsure of what lays ahead then exercising curiosity won't just help uncover answers, it will also help to keep worries at bay.

C - CHILDLIKE – Start channeling your inner five-year-old. Try and see things around you, including any issues on your plate, with fresh eyes. Why is that like that? Why do we do this? Why does it make me feel like this? Try to step away from being the expert and revel in the wonder of seeing things afresh.

U - UNLEARN – Actively challenge what you know. What have you assumed to be true about a situation or topic? Do you really 100% know that is true? What would happen if the opposite were the case? If you're struggling to remove your expert goggles, then phone a friend for a totally fresh view. Grannies are normally good for a wild take on a familiar situation.

R - RELEASE EXPECTATIONS – Let go of expectations about how things will turn out. If Alexander Fleming hadn't let go of the idea of finding an influenza cure, he may never have followed the breadcrumbs that led to the discovery of penicillin.

I - INQUIRY – Ask a lot of questions, preferably open ones. I wonder what…? How would it feel if…? What would happen if…? This will fire your imagination and somewhere in the pile of questions will be some golden, previously unseen answers.

O - OPEN – Open your thinking up to a world of possibilities. Think through all possible outcomes of a situation, even the unlikely seeming ones. Since you don't know 100 per cent what lies ahead and since you don't yet know what is or isn't possible, now is the time to explore all pathways.

U – UNAVOIDABLE – Accept that the messy middle is unavoidable and but also potentially fruitful. Don't rush it but instead give yourself the time and space to process and explore.

S - START SMALL – This is the time to try things out and try things on. Different pathways, different identities, different futures. But start with some small experiments rather than betting the farm straight away.

THE INSPIRATION

Chip Conley, Entrepreneur and Author

Chip Conley is in his late fifties and according to a longevity website that he likes to check, he has at least another forty good years ahead of him. His particular period of reinvention and rebuilding coincided with his early fifties and he has spoken extensively on how mid-life can be a fertile time period for making a transition. Whether you consider yourself mid-life or not, Chip's underlying belief that 'when we stop being a beginner and stop being curious it's all downhill from there' is relevant to all moments of change and transition.

Chip's first 50 years were as a boutique hotel entrepreneur. Aged 26 he got into the business, raising money to buy a run-down San Francisco property where local prostitutes were his best and most loyal customers. With his flair for hospitality this humble start grew into a boutique hotel chain with a rebel ethos under the brand Joie de Vivre with over 3,500 employees and a long list of celebrity guests.

By 2011 Joie de Vivre had grown to over 52 properties, but the recent recession had taken its toll on Chip emotionally and financially and he decided he needed a change. After selling the business he had dedicated two decades of his life to, he found himself feeling adrift, unsure what to do next. Until a CEO came knocking who was young enough to be his son. Brian Chesky, 24-year-old co-founder of Airbnb wanted Chip to mentor him and bring his vast hospitality experience to the fast growing start-up. Chip was most definitely not a digital native. In 2013 he didn't have the Lyft or an Uber app on his phone, had never even heard of the 'sharing economy'. When he first started at Airbnb, surrounded by 25-year-old digital whizz kids, he felt like a fish out of water. There was so much he felt he didn't know that he even doubted his ability to mentor Brian and recast himself as a 'mentern' – part mentor and part intern. He recognized that learning, not just imparting what he knew, would be vital if he was to succeed at this new career crossroads. A short time later Chip was made Airbnb's full time Head of Global Hospitality and Strategy and has been a long-time mentor and adviser to Brian who credits Chip for helping to turn Airbnb into the international hospitality brand that the founder had envisioned. So how did he do it?

First of all, he acknowledged and embraced the messy middle, the neutral zone. He describes it as feeling raw again, noting the disorientation he felt in transforming his identity. 'My word for it? "Gooey." Like what happens in the middle of its metamorphosis into a butterfly.' He had to take off the identity of the expert, the business owner and the CEO in order to find a new role for this next stage of his life. Secondly, alongside his experience and wisdom, Chip's lack of Silicon Valley knowledge led to a curiosity which proved invaluable. He says: 'I was able to stoke a fire by being catalytically curious... My beginner's mind helped us to see a few of our blind spots a little better, as my mind was free of the habits of being the expert.' Chip's lack of digital knowledge deterred him from focusing on the tech and helped him to focus on the hosts and the guests who were the beating heart of the Airbnb model. He asked the daft questions, the obvious questions, the ones that no-one had asked. 'Why should hosts, who are not employees, care about the quality of the guest experience? Why is our review system the way it is? What if we more directly linked the quality of the host performance to their search ranking?' (Conley, 2018).

Chip's powerful blend of experience and curiosity enabled him to provide business-defining advice to Brian Chesky and the Airbnb team for over four years. He now works as a powerful advocate and support for people making big transitions, in particular during mid-life, through a centre called The Modern Elder Academy. All founded on his belief that 'Curiosity opens up while wisdom edits down.'

Conclusion

While we would prefer to know what lies around every corner, it is simply impossible to plan for everything that lays ahead. If we want to leave a setback behind and embark on a journey to somewhere better, then we need to embrace the idea of getting lost for a while. Not only is a messy middle period inevitable but it is where all the great new ideas and plans emerge. So, if you are feeling lost and unsure of what comes next, just remember that it worked for David Bowie so it must be good!

CHAPTER EIGHT

The unfair reputation of taking it slowly

'If I allow myself to slow down, I'm wasting time. I'll just start rolling backwards and never kick into gear again' – what we tell ourselves shortly before we crash and burn.

On slowing down. Speed of success is too often used as a benchmark in evaluating potential. This chapter focuses on the importance of slowing down and even stopping in order to move forwards again.

Myth – If it didn't happen yesterday, it's never going to happen.

Truth – The virtue of patience and value of inaction.

Most of us will instinctively feel when the time has come to slow down. Just before a holiday when we are barely functioning humans, or crawling to the finish line of Friday afternoon as our proverbial hamster wheel is spinning out of control. It could also be when things are moving slowly, but in the wrong direction. But do we ever slow down or stop when we feel the time has come to take stock? Of course not. We do quite the opposite. We launch ourselves like an incoming missile towards our physical and mental demise.

Myth

Working hard and not slowing down has become a benchmark and superior way of being for many societies. It's how you prove yourself to be a useful and successful member of your community.

You can trace this sentiment all the way back to the Bible which elevates the constant business of ants above human idleness:

> Go to the ant, you sluggard; consider its ways and be wise! It has no commander, no overseer or ruler, yet it stores its provisions in summer and gathers its food at harvest. How long will you lie there, you sluggard? When will you get up from your sleep? A little sleep, a little slumber, a little folding of the hands to rest – and poverty will come on you like a thief and scarcity like an armed man. (Proverbs 6: 6–11, *King James Bible*).

In the 16th century, John Calvin and Martin Luther further perpetuated this work ethic through the Protestant Reformation, celebrating good work as a sign of faith and salvation. When Europe became too comfortable, the Puritans set sail for America, founding the American dream around even more self-discipline and work. And so the threat of eternal damnation sowed the seeds for our modus operandi to this day: the more you do, the more successful you'll become. And the faster you do it, the greater the kudos for effort and achievement.

The myth of achievement at pace, without slowing down or resting – or heaven forbid stopping all together – further gained momentum through unhelpful mantras by 19th century luminaries such as Thomas Edison, who widely proclaimed sleep as a waste of time (despite taking lengthy naps each day himself) and Winston Churchill's famous words 'I never worry about action, but only inaction'.

Mark Zuckerberg isn't far behind, with 'Move fast and break things. Unless you're breaking things, you're not moving fast enough.' This battle cry of Silicon Valley has, it seems, become the battle cry of the 21st century. Whether you work in tech or teach primary school. At speed is more desirable than in your own time.

The thing is, while you can break circuit boards and code and simply put them back together, it's not always so straightforward with humans. We break easily. And we repair harder.

Yet regular slowing down periods can make all the difference and it has been proven many times over just how interconnected rest and performance are.

US President William Howard Taft suggested back in 1910 that every American worker needed two to three months of vacation a year 'in order to continue his work next year with the energy and effectiveness that it ought to have.' The U.S. legislators didn't see it that way and to this day, US workers are not legally entitled to paid holiday. On the other side of the pond, Europe has largely embraced the need and benefits of paid time off, with Germany, France, Sweden and the UK offering an average of five paid weeks a year (Dishman, 2018).

And despite this right protected by law, Britons still wasted 163 million annual leave days in 2016 with the average UK employee failing to use up to five days of annual leave per year. Ironically, 36 per cent of workers polled cited having 'too much on at work to take time off' as their reason for not utilizing their full holiday allowance (HR News, 2017).

That's for the big breaks, what about the small ones? We don't fare that much better at them. Office workers in the UK tend to take only 16 minutes a day to eat their lunch break, usually dining at their desk. Definitely a case of lunch over break (Hall, 2019).

We really don't seem very good at taking breaks! Could this be the reason why, compared with the rest of the G7 countries, the UK consistently presents a long running productivity gap? (ONS, 2018).

For those of us fearing the wrath of our bosses, it's not like they don't recognize the benefits of a breather. A US study by Oxford Economics has shown that most managers recognize the benefits of taking time away from work as it provides employees with higher productivity, stronger workplace morale, greater employee retention, and significant health benefits (Oxford Economics, 2014).

And this is why, despite our deep-rooted feelings of guilt or ineptitude, it is vital that we embrace the value and opportunity of taking our foot off the pedal from time to time. There are very real benefits to slowing and stopping. Because, what that gives us in return, is recovery, perspective, and fuel. We've just never really talked about this concept through the metric we collectively care about and respect: progress.

Truth

It's no surprise that the ever-forward thinking Ariana Huffington, co-founder of the *Huffington Post* and founder and CEO of Thrive Global, has already done a re-brand on rest. Her suggestion was to not call it 'down time', but 'thrive time'. As Arianna shared with *Your Brain at Work* podcast, recharging after strenuous bouts of work shouldn't be considered a luxury, so fundamental are they to how we set ourselves up for success. This comes hot off the Gallup Report 2020 polls that show burnout has become a national problem (Gallup, 2020). Approximately 23 per cent of the nearly 7,500 full-time employees surveyed said they were always or very often burned out (Weller, 2019).

An interesting perspective is also offered by Tony Schwartz and Catherine McCarthy in their *Harvard Business Review* paper 'Manage your energy, not your time'. They conducted a now famous study among Wachovia employees in the US which found that when people take regular breaks, they are measurably more productive. The study concluded with a recommendation of focusing on these four energy renewal spaces to give your mind and body the optimum amount of R&R: physical energy, emotional energy, mental energy and spiritual energy (Schwartz and McCarthy, 2007). Focusing on energy (which each of us can dial up or down and are in control of) versus time (a finite and inflexible quantity) is a really good way of thinking about time off and the value it creates for time on.

Back to the rest of us.

The truth, as convenient or inconvenient as it may be, is that slowing down and stopping for a while will make you stronger, more resilient, healthier and happier. Kids do it instinctively. When they're tired, they take a nap. When they're stuck with a problem, they stop and step away for a bit. When they're sick, they make sure to request time off school to recover. Without guilt. Without FOMO.

Athletes are great at slowing down, or tapering, too. Regular rest intervals, engineered periods of recovery are all carefully calibrated to perform at your best when required. The idea of only ever ploughing full steam ahead without decreasing your speed would seem as idiotic as doing nothing at all and still expecting to excel.

Here's another way of illustrating the point, exemplified through the act of weightlifting. When you lift weights, you stress your muscles. This stress creates tiny tears in your muscle tissue. These knit back together stronger as you let your arms recover. It's the recovery process that helps rebuild the tissue back stronger. Not just the stress you place your muscles under at the gym. Stress without recovery would injure and damage your muscles. Recovery helps us grow.

That is why creatine (a popular sports supplement), when consumed in larger quantities, is considered a performance enhancing drug and is a banned substance for competing athletes. Precisely because of how it works: it helps muscles recover more quickly during exercise. Again, recovery is a competitive advantage. Recovery helps us grow. In fact, recovery is an undisputed precursor to performance.

While it's easier to accept forced physical recovery (because your body will simply prevent you from continuing), it's much harder to give your head a break. Not least because enforced mental rest periods are arguably harder to quantify and therefore still considered a 'soft tool' when it comes to looking after ourselves and our business. But the principle applies to both. So it's doubly important to discover the best intervals of recovery for your body and mind. And feeling good about it!

THE TOOL

The pressure puncture

The secret of taking it slowly and affording your body and mind the right amount of respite is often the missing ingredient to rebuilding from our work and life setbacks. Most of us 'do' weekends and holidays. But we often crawl to the finish line, exhausted by marathon weeks and months without space to think or gain perspective. And, of course, who doesn't spend the first half of their holiday ill? We neglect the necessary pause button in our daily routines. We should be thinking of temporary pauses every day, multiple times a day, depending on the challenge at hand.

The 'pressure puncture' as illustrated in Figure 7.1 is a way of thinking about when and for how long to slow down. Everybody experiences pressure and stress differently. What might be a doddle for you, could be a D-Day for me. And something what takes me a quick walk down to the coffee shop to recover from, could cause somebody to take a full day's rest. We're all different. This tool is meant to help us compartmentalize different types of recovery strategies, or different modes of 'slow'. The important thing is to implement both daily and periodic rests. They work on different levels and for different situations. Consciously taking breaks becomes especially important in a 'working from home' environment, where the benefit of less interruption also means the drawback of more sedentary work. It's easy to spend all day in the same room and clock up no more than 20 steps a day.

FIGURE 8.1   Finding your pace with the pressure puncture

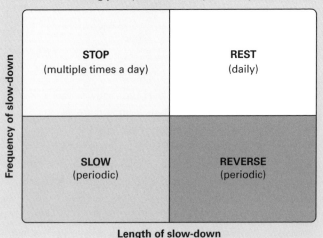

STOP:

- Multiple, short breaks taken throughout the day
- Time to change the scenery, stretch your legs, disconnect from a task
- Hydrate, snack, get some fresh air, strike up a conversation with a colleague or friend

Objective: Recharge, optimize your energy for the next task, finish the day less exhausted and grumpy and able to enjoy your after hours.

REST:

- Daily down time that feels like a proper time out! Could be a visit to the gym, watching Netflix with the family, cooking dinner, walking the dog, meditating… more than a quick break in between meetings, and less than a longer down period

Objective: Gain some perspective on the day ahead or the day that has been, uninterrupted down time that allows you to fully disconnect from demands and stresses, space to regain control and set priorities.

SLOW:

- Longer breaks or a period of time over which you take it easier than usual
- Could be after a particularly stressful period at work or draining personal experience
- Give yourself more time to do less with chunks of free time in between

Objective: Overcome exhaustion and prevent burnout, enough time to re-establish healthy habits that may have fallen by the wayside during a stressful period, minimize the pressure you feel and experience to give yourself time to recalibrate.

REVERSE:

- A change in direction, characterized by stopping and rewinding

- An intervention for when your modus operandi is counterproductive to moving forwards happily and sustainably

- Take away the pressure of an instinctive quick fix with instant results and allow yourself to deconstruct your way of thinking, habits, and goals. Then rebuild your framework

Objective: To give yourself the space and time to rewire your approach to life and work. This isn't about getting it done quickly, but about doing it right and in a sustainable manner. The goal is to change some fundamentals, unlearn bad habits and build back stronger.

THE INSPIRATION

Tom Hodgkinson, Editor of *The Idler*:

Tom has always loved the idea of being in control of his own time. His corporate life as a journalist, working for a newspaper, didn't give him what he was looking for. He was forever busy without the time or control to 'think deeply about what you're doing and where you're going'. Tom likes a lie in, to read – a lot, have a beer in the evening, potter and do work in intensive intervals, so that he has free time to explore other things of interest. He cares deeply about the question 'how do you live' and 'how do you work'. He isn't by any means work shy. He just doesn't subscribe to the idea of presenteeism, working yourself to death to climb the corporate ladder, nor does he believe that you can do more after 10 hours at your desk than after four. As he observed, would you want a surgeon to perform a procedure on you at the end of their 12-hour shift? In fact, society's obsession with productivity at speed is, Tom observes, discriminatory towards older people, people with disabilities or towards people with responsibilities outside of or within a 9–5 working environment. And so Tom took his commitment and conviction around having time to slow down and answer these bigger questions in life one step further than most of us would and founded a magazine dedicated to the subject of idling. Fittingly, he called it *The Idler*. The Idler promises to devote itself to 'helping people to lead more fulfilled lives. We publish a bi-monthly magazine, produce online courses and run live events. We want you to Slow Down, Have Fun and Live Well!' The Idler and the courses that have spun-off of this philosophy advocate a good dose of idling every day. In fact, Tom strongly believes that you should enjoy your everyday life to the extent of not necessarily wanting or needing to go on holiday! One of the benefits of idling include a better ability to conceive and execute visions for your business and life. You're less slave to productivity for productivity's sake, and are more purposeful in your time and energy and direction. Which, in turn, makes you more efficient. So if you haven't embraced idling so far, now is your chance to give it a go and feel totally legit!

Our next inspiration comes from Nick who has identified quantifiable benefits to slowing down and resting. Following a medical emergency, Nick turned this recovery strategy into a life and work philosophy. And, like Tom, a business.

Nick Propper, CEO of Impact Human Performance:

A few years ago, Nick noticed his wedding band feeling a little tighter around his finger. Then he noticed the elasticated bit of his sock leaving deep rings around his leg. Not long after, his whole body began to blow up like a balloon. A trip to the doctor's confirmed Nick was moments away from a heart attack and was in the midst of suffering kidney failure. He'd been ignoring the warning signs for months. Work was busy and it was inconvenient to think something might be wrong. Nick was put on medication and started to feel better. So he continued his busy schedule as if nothing had happened. But he wasn't going to get away with it. Not long after, he started to feel depressed. Really depressed. And this time he knew he needed to change something. A serendipitous training course he went on turned him on to the idea of thinking about the importance of human performance through the lens of energy. How can people manage their energy better in work and in life? It wasn't something many companies were talking about at the time. Certainly not something that most of us would come across during our professional development hours at work. But it struck a nerve with Nick and he decided this was what he wanted to do: learn and teach on the subject of getting more energy.

Nick observed:

We're obsessed with time and efficiency. We see time as value creation. We talk and learn about time management. Being busy is a badge of honour. And utilization is the currency in too many organizations. In addition to this, we should be talking about the management of energy. Because time in the absence of energy is low value. If you're not controlling your energy, someone else will.

Nick is now co-founder of Impact Human Performance, an organization that coaches individuals and companies to better manage their energy and that of their staff. Nick wants to move people's perceptions around this topic away from being soft skills that are nice to have and turn them into a business-critical investment case.

> It's always about performance. This isn't some hippy dippy adventure. We want to set people up to sustain doing well rather than having to pull back. We want to grow resilience. And recovery is a crucial component of resilience and performance. It's important to intentionally pause throughout the day. Weekends and annual leave aren't enough. Hourly recovery mechanisms throughout the day should be our strategic response to stress and maintaining a good balance. And it can absolutely be about very small things. It's not about boiling the ocean with changes. In fact, boiling the ocean is the biggest barrier to improving your performance. Reminding yourself to drink an extra glass of water at work to avoid that 4pm headache you keep getting means you arrive home in a better mood, happier to engage with your family and enjoy your down time.

Conclusion

We are riddled with guilt when it comes to taking a break. Will it make us look lazy? Will we come across as less ambitious. Will the people who don't take as many breaks achieve more than I will today? These worries are based on century-long myths and unhelpful standards. Not only are you entitled to breaks, but they will make you rebuild better, stronger, and faster.

CHAPTER NINE

All paths lead through failure

'I failed and now I feel like a failure.' An all-too-common
thought after something has gone to awry.

On failure. Each success is propped up by the many
failures that came before. This chapter examines failure as a prerequisite to progress and the ways in which you
can use it to move forwards.

> **Myth** – Failure happens to people who don't succeed.
> **Truth** – Failure is a critical part of progress.

Dolly Parton once lost a Dolly Parton lookalike contest,
which is the best evidence that failure sometimes just
happens (Chang and Thompson, 2012). Failure isn't on

anyone's bucket list. We don't walk away from something that has gone awry and think 'What a great result. I'm feeling super pumped. Well done me.' We register it as a loss, a lesson, something to be avoided and not repeated. Yet if you are considering a rebuild then it is most likely because something in your life or work has faltered or failed in some way. So how can we move past failures and towards something better down the line? In this chapter we examine failures as prerequisites to progress and ways we can feel less awful about them, possibly even start feeling positive about them.

Myth

We are surrounded by failure. Over 40 per cent of marriages end in divorce (ONS, 2016). 25 per cent of start-ups close in the first year and 60 per cent within the first three years (Gov.uk, 2019). And 80 per cent of all new product launches in grocery stores fail (Nielsen, 2018). We are even surrounded by stories of failures that turned out to be successes at a later date. Walt Disney was fired from his first job at a Kansas City newspaper because his editor felt he 'lacked imagination and had no good ideas' (Connors and Smith, 2014). Anna Wintour was let go from her job as a junior fashion editor at *Harper's Bazaar* only 12 years before she was made Editor in Chief at *Vogue* (Moss, 2015).

So if it is so common, why do we fear and avoid it so much? Why does the thought of failing send chills down the spine of most sane and sensible folks? And what can we do to move past the negative impact that a failure can leave on us?

It helps to understand why we dislike it so much, and this is partly down to how brains work. Have you ever stayed in a bad relationship or job because you worried that it would be worse leaving? Have you ever not had a crack at something you wanted to do because you worried you might fail? Some of this is thanks to our little grey cells because our brains are wired to avoid situations where there is a risk of failure or loss. The recognized term for this is 'loss aversion' and it is a form of cognitive bias, a systematic but sometimes flawed way that our brains make decisions. Quite simply our brains really don't like the idea of losing things. So much so that losses loom far larger in our minds that gains of an equal size. For example researchers have shown that we dislike losing £100 far more than we enjoy gaining £100 (Kahneman and Tversky, 1979). As a result, we are wired to avoid losing things in whatever way possible even when the risk of failure might be much smaller than the risk of having a really great, winning outcome.

Avoiding losses is undoubtedly useful in stopping us making outlandish and risky decisions. It says no to betting the house and car on red. It says no eloping to Gretna Green with the person you met on the train yesterday. But loss aversion can also stop us making positive, well thought through decisions because the fear of loss and risk is too high. Yet many of life's really valuable and important decisions that are worth taking have some element of risk attached to them. This is where that fear of failure and the resulting loss holds us back from taking a great but slightly scary new job. From settling down in a good relationship for fear of losing our single life. From trying again at a business venture if it went wrong the first time. A recent study into global entrepreneurship showed that around one-third of would-be entrepreneurs don't even venture to start a business because of fear of failure (Global Entrepreneurship Monitor, 2021). No wonder then that if someone has experienced business failure or loss that they would avoid ever doing it again for fear of disaster repeating.

So if we are wired to fear failure in the first place then maybe we shouldn't be too tough on ourselves if we don't feel like jumping back on the horse after something has gone awry in life or work. If we take a chance and it doesn't go as planned, then the impact on our mindset can be huge. Just try to remember it's the little grey cells causing our fear and worry to dial up.

It is also very common to worry that if something has gone wrong that it may go wrong again. After all that's just a sensible way of learning from our mistakes isn't it? Or is it? Again we need to keep an eye on how our brains make sense of things. Humans are pattern-seeking creatures. We just love to digest events and info and to make sense of them. It is this wonderful pattern finding and sense making ability that helps us learn and make judgements as a species. Age four we ate those weird red berries at the end of the garden when no-one was looking. We got really sick, so we didn't do it again! When we poked our brother in the eye he cried, but when we hugged him he liked it. So poking is out and hugging is in. Patterns help make order out of chaos. They tell us not to eat yellow snow and to step in front of fast-moving cars. But human brains are so good at seeing patterns that we even see them when they aren't really there and this can lead us to seeing things that don't exist. Conspiracy theories, superstitions and seeing faces in clouds are all examples of this. Are those red pants really helping you pass exams? If you feature on the cover of *Sports Illustrated* will the 'Sports Illustrated jinx' strike you and your career take a turn for the worse? Did someone really see the face of Jesus in a tomato? Probably not. More likely these are random acts and isolated incidents that our brains have woven into neat patterns to create a sense making story out of them.

We can do the same with failures. If we experience something going wrong and the sting and shame of a loss then we weave it into a story. It wasn't a random chance, it was a lesson to be learned and a sign of what will happen if we try again. If at first you didn't succeed, it will fail next time. We are a failure. Yet sometimes failures are just a random occurrence in your story line. They aren't a portent of more problems to come or indicators of future failure. They are just a single, disappointing occurrence that we shouldn't weave a narrative pattern around or make too much of.

Nowhere is this better understood than in the world of sport where winning or losing is a regular occurrence with score sheets showing binary wins or losses. Jamil Qureshi is a world renowned sports psychologist who has helped six elite sportspeople reach number one in the world in their chosen field. He believes that fear of failure is one of the biggest inhibitors to success and reaching peak performance and that much of this fear is totally unfounded. He jokes that fear stands for False Evidence Appearing Real. That much of the time we allow fear of things that aren't even going to happen to hold us back from doing what we want to do. He also warns not to build failures into a narrative of failure and not to see a pattern where there isn't one. 'A golfer is aiming to be number one in the world in two years' time. If he loses one match does that loss say anything about his ability to meet his long-term ambition? Does a loss today have any bearing on his long-term success? Absolutely not.' (Qureshi, 2021).

In fact he goes further to encourage us to see a positive connection between failure and success. We are born into the world not knowing how to do very much and the only way we will learn and develop is by repeatedly failing until we succeed. He believes that failure is part-payment for success. 'The price of success is always pain in full and upfront. If we want to develop and grow then it is vital to make a positive connection between the two. We simply can't develop and get better if we aren't prepared to fail and fail repeatedly.' (Qureshi, 2020).

Truth

So it seems that failure is unavoidable. Sometimes it just happens and we shouldn't read too much into it as a reflection of our chances of success next time round. Elizabeth Taylor knew this when she got married no less than seven times! So apart from getting used to the fact that failures are an inevitable part of life and work, how else should we be trying to process and move on from them? Should we just ignore them and keep on plugging away the way we were before?

Helpfully, many people have studied how we can positively view failure in order to help future performance. The leader in this field is an incredible woman called Dr Carol Dweck. She often focuses on childhood as this is the period in our lives where we fail and learn the most and she coined the now widely accepted concept of 'growth mindset' (Dweck, 2006). Over many years of study Dr Dweck identified two mindsets that play a huge part in successful growth and development in children and equally can apply to adults. Those with a 'fixed mindset' believe that their talent and intellect is fixed and can't be developed. They were born smart and talented or not, and that's the hand they have been dealt. Conversely, those with a growth mindset believe that their intellect and talent can be developed through practice and hard work. The interesting thing for rebuilders is the different attitudes to failure that come with these mindsets. Fixed mindset people tend towards proving and documenting their abilities. Tests and exams are seen as ways of validating their talents rather than as opportunities to develop them. They do not respond well to failure, feeling that it validates the fixed limits of their skills. People with growth mindsets respond very differently. Tough tests and other challenges are embraced as welcome chances to learn and grow. If they fail or mess up then it is a sign they are challenging themselves, learning and getting smarter. This growth mindset creates a real love of learning and an inbuilt resilience to failure. In one test Carol gave ten-year-old children some tests that were slightly too tricky for them. The children with a growth mindset relished the challenge. Those with a fixed mindset were devastated when they didn't do well.

Not only were they devastated at the failure but in further studies they said that they would go to great lengths to avoid another failure. Some said they would cheat next time instead of studying more (Source 16) or try to find someone who did worse than them so they could feel better (Source 17).

The good news is that we can all develop a growth mindset. By reframing our challenges and limitations as opportunities to learn and develop we can lessen the impact that setbacks have on us. We build resilience to challenge and feel more willing to stretch ourselves outside our comfort zone and into the space where we can learn and grow. One tactic is to reframe how we emotionally respond to things we struggle with or can't crack. Rather than feel defeated, we can try to see the frustration as a sign of learning and getting better. Just the act of finding something challenging means that our brains are forming new neural pathways and getting improving. Language can help with this and Dr Dweck recommends adopting the language of 'not yet'. It isn't that you can't do something, simply that you don't know how to do it yet. It isn't that the idea was a flop, it just isn't quite right yet. Time and time again this simple approach of reframing the language around and meaning of struggle and failure, has proven to improve performance (Nussbaum and Dweck, 2008).

Alongside changing our mindset to be more 'growth' and less 'fixed', what else is there that we can do to progress beyond struggle and failure? Is there a way that we can ensure that the development opportunities do result in development? We have all been told that doing the same thing again and again is the definition of madness, so how can we try to learn from failures while not getting too hung up on them? Just failing and then blindly moving onto the next thing isn't the best approach. Improvements are more likely when we seek to actively learn from what has gone wrong before. Countless research studies have looked at how entrepreneurs do or don't learn from business failures and show that failing fast and then simply getting up and going again isn't the answer. One study tracked an entrepreneur's five failed businesses over 20 years and proved that although the causes varied, all the failures had similarities. The entrepreneur hadn't learned from previous mistakes and the study concluded that learning from failure doesn't happen automatically but requires careful and deliberate reflection on what has gone wrong (Pretorius and Roux, 2011).

If we want to look at how we can individually improve then it is useful to look at what the best in the world do in order to be the best. How do elite sports people and musicians become the elite? Is it enough to scrape away at a violin or wildly swing at tennis balls while thinking 'this is a great development opportunity' or is there a little more to it? Turns out there is a little more to it and it is called 'deliberate practice' (Ericsson and Harwell, 2019). Deliberate practice is an approach to improving performance that can be observed in the training regimes of elite performers. Rather than just repeating the same thing again and again, deliberate practice is about focused and concentrated learning efforts. Exploring weaknesses in a game or technique, breaking them down into small chunks, then mindfully focusing on practising one piece at a time.

It requires concentration and focus and also feedback to review whether that particular chunk is getting better. Examples include professional chess players practise technique of removing certain pieces to repeatedly practise the endgame with only certain pieces still in play. Or musicians playing and replaying the same small section of a piece of music.

This approach is transferable to almost anything we want to get better at, even if we aren't aiming for a word record any time soon. For example, if your aim is to handle conflict or difficult conversations better, then begin by replaying the last couple of conversations of this nature. Carefully think through each part before, during and after. What could have gone better? What might you try next time? What one thing will you focus on? This part is critical. Rather than a vague goal of 'be better next time', keep it focused on one small improvement such as 'enter the room calmer by taking three deep breaths before I go in'. Then really concentrate on that one action next time you see your boss, ex-spouse or difficult client. Then reflect back on your progress, select another focused area for practiced improvement and repeat. It means getting off auto pilot and really thinking about the small things that you want to improve. The idea is to keep chalking up small, continuous improvements week after week. If you keep improving and stick at it then imagine the progress that can be made over a year or two.

THE TOOL

Alongside working on our mindset to try to view failures as development opportunities, we can take practical steps to improve our outcomes next time round. Here is a tool based around the concept of deliberate practice that can be applied to almost all aspects of life where we want to see our performance improve. From writing, presenting and productivity, to sports, cooking and relationships, great strides can be made with sustained effort and concentration. We are going to use the example of working towards being a better presenter, a goal which many people struggle with.

Deliberate practice steps

1 Set a goal

Be crystal clear about what it is you want work on and improve. Keeping in mind why this is important to you, and what it will look like when you get there, will keep you focused and motivated.

eg Feeling confident and well equipped when giving large presentations to staff at events such as company meetings.

2 Separate into chunks

Break down the entire process in steps from beginning to end and then decide where to focus first.

eg Preparation of material is the first focus. The visual slides are strong but the delivery could be improved.

3 Small improvements

Get a sense of what 'better' looks like for this particular chunk and then repeat multiple times with a careful eye on repeatedly improving the area of particular focus.

eg Watching some excellent TED Talks provides clues that the pace needs to be slowed right down with a slower speaking rate and more pauses and breaths. Deliver the voice-over multiple times with this in mind.

4 Stay focused

The more times we do something the easier it is to slip into autopilot but mindlessness doesn't lead to improvements. Keep the practice 'deliberate'.

eg When working on the delivery, really note when to take breaths and how it feels in your body to slow down and take longer pauses.

5 Seek feedback

Create a feedback loop to carefully review your progress – another person, a recording, a score sheet. Any method will work as long as you refer back to it repeatedly to see how you are progressing and what else can be tweaked.

eg Ask a friend to sit in and listen and give feedback, or record yourself and listen back noting what still needs work. When you next give a presentation in public, have a friendly ear on standby to provide feedback to assess your progress.

INSPIRATION

A dyslexic can't write a book. In fact a dyslexic can barely write a shopping list. At least that's the story that Sara has told herself since discovering she was dyslexic aged 20.

Yet here I am writing a book. The journey that got me here is a cautionary tale of how creating limiting stories and beliefs around failures can hold you back, and how shaking them off can set you free.

The way I discovered my dyslexia is almost too comical to be true. After many months of swotting and entry exams I got into the prestigious Oxford University to study English Literature. I had always been a hard-working student, but my work was oddly sloppy, messy and careless. Teachers nagged me that if I 'just knuckled down and applied myself' I could go far.

Then I started university. The reading overwhelmed me, the essays bemused me and I was failing. One term in, I wrote an essay on the concept of failure in literature and somewhat ironically spelled the word as 'failiure' about a zillion times. At this point a wise tutor suggested I might actually be dyslexic and as preposterous as that sounded it turned out to be true.

After getting tested and having the diagnosis confirmed I felt utterly defeated. No amount of knuckling down and applying myself was going to help me as I dragged myself through three years of miserable study that I felt was terminally beyond me. I was a failure, my degree was a disaster and my confidence was shattered. I had gone from feeling like a good student to believing I would be a disastrous adult who would struggle in the world of work. And so I carried what I perceived as my 'failure' into my working life.

Being dyslexic and being sub-par at certain things, particularly long-form writing, became part of the story I told myself. It became a stumbling block that I was certain I couldn't get over. I would let people at work know I was dyslexic before they judged me on errors in my emails or written work. I shied away from writing like the plague. I lived in terror of being asked to write long-hand awards papers and would proclaim loudly to my bosses that I was dyslexic and can't write a sentence so don't even try me. Was this true? Partly. But not entirely. I can write. I'm just not great and it takes me more wailing and gnashing of teeth than other people. Yet I held on tight to this story because it helped me avoid the thing I felt useless at and helped me avoid further failures. But this story also held me back. I didn't win awards for papers I didn't write. I didn't write articles when my peers stepped up to do it and, crucially, I abandoned trying to consciously practise and improve my writing. I gave up trying to get better and rolled over in defeat.

Until I met someone who just refused to believe my take on the disaster. My co-author Anna Vogt proffered that of course we could write a book, despite my many protestations to the contrary. As a former professional athlete, she saw things differently. Yes, I found it hard and it takes me ages (and I hate it by the way!), but she believed that with practise and perseverance my writing wasn't a write off. So after 25 years of telling myself and others that I can't even hold a pen, I am writing this book. I am tackling something that isn't easy but also isn't as impossible as I had always told myself. As I have ploughed in the hours painfully writing and rewriting chapters, I have noticed that my writing has got better. Turns out that practice really does work. Makes me wonder how much better it would be if I hadn't abandoned all hope and effort 25 years ago!

Conclusion

It is understandable to feel deflated after something we have poured our energy into falls flat, but one failure doesn't mean we won't succeed next time around; in fact, quite the opposite. Failures are necessary steps on the path to improvement and success. Plus with deliberate practise we can get better at just about anything we set our mind to.

CHAPTER TEN

Flexibility will fix it

'Changing your mind is for people without a strong opinion.' – what we've been conditioned to think when change sweeps in.

On changing your mind. Society has conditioned us to think that changing our minds is a sign of indecision and inconsistency. This chapter examines how, quite frankly, the opposite can be true.

Myth – To be confident and strong you must stick to your guns no matter what.
Truth – Changing your mind is a sign of a good listener, a confident thinker and an empowering leader.

'But you've just changed your mind!' Who hasn't had this hurled at them like an insult from the age of, say, five years old? Whether the topic in question concerns your choice for an after-school treat or the preference of a candidate you are about to hire (or not), going back on an opinion you have made feels more painful than proceeding with the wrong decision. Years ago, Anna was sitting in a creative review. And it was the night before a big presentation. This would have been the fifth or sixth time the group in the room was revising the same ideas, scripts and print concepts. Everyone had been over them and collectively agreed that this was what was going to be presented to the clients the next day. Suddenly, a niggle of doubt started to creep into someone's mind. After having looked through everything for the umpteenth time, wasn't one of the ideas actually off brief and a bit similar to something a competitor had just done? It had seemed a familiar concept from the get-go, but it took all this time for that niggle to fully mature into a doubt and now a full-blown veto. Wouldn't it be much better to rewrite the whole idea? The presiding CEO in the room nearly flew off the handle and challenged the doubter right back 'Well, you've seen this before and you didn't suggest changing it then. It's a bit late now. We should just stick with it,' to which the person in question replied, 'The fact I didn't say anything yesterday doesn't change the fact it's still wrong today. We need to change it.' And reconstruct the idea we did, through the wee hours of the morning, because the alternative would have had us looking ignorant.

Myth

Think about the last time you changed your mind. How did you feel? Nervous? Indecisive? Judged? Now think about the last time someone you know changed their mind? How did that make you feel about them? Frustrated? That they got it wrong? Or maybe you were impressed?

If you're someone who easily embraces changing your mind and applauds others who do the same, well done. Your adaptability is commendable. You may now skip on to the next chapter. For everyone else who feels even a modicum of unease, sit tight. This one is for you.

As with so many behaviours we tackle in this book, a flexible mindset that readily adapts and pivots isn't something we are naturally blessed with. There are some scientific reasons for this, such as confirmation bias and loss aversion, and many more centuries worth of learnt behaviours that put it into practise. The consequences of which become more and more burdensome on our society, progress, and on our personal happiness as the years tick on. Our negativity towards mental flexibility is derived not just from how we feel about ourselves but also, and more viscerally, how we fear others think of us. Will they think that we got it wrong? That we are incapable of sticking to our guns? That we don't have a strong enough opinion or clear goal?

In 1965, the eminent Canadian–American economist John Kenneth Galbraith penned a book review for *The New York Times* of John Maynard Keynes's famous work *The General Theory of Employment, Interest and Money* (Keynes, 1936). Galbraith discussed the slow acceptance in the US of Keynes's economic theories. He highlighted the changing perspective of economist Alvin H. Hansen who had criticized Keynes's previous book *A Treatise on Money* (Keynes, 1930).

Of this resistance, Galbraith observed: 'Faced with the choice between changing one's mind and proving that there is no need to do so, almost everyone gets busy on the proof.' (Galbraith, 1965).

While Galbraith was referring to the debate on economic theories, this very observant quip will no doubt strike a nerve with most of us. According to research conducted by psychology experts at Queen's University in Canada, the average person will have more than 6,200 thoughts in a single day (Craig, 2020). It's hard to imagine that all of these thoughts are immovably set in stone and won't eventually evolve, change or be overruled by new stimulus.

But still. It's hard to change. And such is our reluctance to alter our established way of thinking that some people are turning to alternative ways of cracking this neurological code with the help of psychedelics. Michael Pollan, author of *How to Change Your Mind* suggests that the use of psychedelics and LSD can aid in the process of ego-dissolution which separates how we integrate what's happening to us in any given moment, with our abiding sense of who we are (Pollan, 2018). And what this seems to lead to is the creation of new connections temporarily forming in our brain. These new connections produce new insights, new perspectives and new ways of looking at the world. The feeling amongst scientists is that these chemicals allow us to essentially reboot our brain. If the brain is stuck in narrow grooves of thought, all these deep groves are temporarily suspended in a way that allows us to break those patterns. Pollan argues that while psychedelics have gained the reputation of 'making you crazy', his research has shown that in the right doses in the right environments they can actually 'make you sane'.

Just to be clear, this isn't an endorsement of drug use, rather an interesting observation on what it sometimes takes to break free from the convenient and well-versed status quo.

Truth

But some of us are already there. Fully fledged advocates of mental gymnastics. Like Derek Sivers, founder of CD Baby, once put it: 'I love it when I think the opposite today of what I thought when I woke up this morning. To me, there's no feeling better than that; when I actually changed my mind or have my mind changed on a subject. That is amazing. That's my favourite thing in life.' (Foroux, 2020).

Because it's not very often that we are complimented on changing tack, it's really liberating to hear people talk with enthusiasm about the benefits of adapting their point of view, based on new information and experiences.

President Barack Obama famously claimed at the Museum of African American History in celebration of Nelson Mandela's birthday: 'I change my mind all the time based on facts.' (Obama, 2019).

What's important to consider in this process is that flexibility of mind and action should be deliberate and considered and designed to improve the outcome you are hoping to achieve, not to simply please stakeholders or compensate for a lack of conviction.

In a day-to-day reality where change is our constant companion, anyone who runs a business or household managing people or children will know that nothing ever quite happens as it was planned for. You'll think differently about kids in restaurants once you become a parent. Your point of view on diversity, or the lack thereof, may have been challenged through the aftermath of the George Floyd murder in 2020. Once someone close to you falls seriously ill, you will think differently about your life's priorities. Being able to respond to changes constructively, being able to see a point of view from a perspective that differs from our own immediate thoughts is not always easy. But we do it all the time. But when you consider how quickly these life and lived experiences turn our perspectives upside down, how sure can we, or should we ever be? There is always a different side, a different experience, a different solution.

Dick Fosbury was one such person who didn't let the status quo get in his way. Dick was an American high jumper who, contrary to the popular practise of jumping over the bar forwards, explored and perfected the technique of using the last four or five steps before the jump to run in a curve and then jump over the bar backwards. This approach allowed the athlete to lean into his turn, away from the bar, resulting in the centre of gravity to be lowered even before knee flexion, giving a longer time period for the take-off thrust. Additionally, on take-off, the sudden move from inward lean to outwards produced a rotation of the jumper's body along the bar's axis, aiding clearance. Thanks to his ability to quite literally embrace a flexible mindset, Dick jumped higher than any of his competitors, resulting in a gold medal win at the 1968 Mexico City Olympics (Williams, 2018).

Digging in our heels and standing our ground is, contrary to popular belief and glamorization of this behaviour, often easier to do than to evolve one's position. Why? Because one approach requires you to think, evaluate, re-think, and resolve differing perspectives whereas the other one requires you to do well... nothing. Now every so often the right decision is to stand firm and not to budge. Such as refusing to be bullied by a client, or accepting lesser pay for a job than a counterpart. But inflexibility should be based on your unwavering commitment to achieving the right outcome for yourself and others.

And let's not forget the reciprocal effect that opening one's mind has. If you show willingness to listen, engage, evaluate and accommodate someone else's point of view where appropriate, they will feel more confident in doing the same for you or the next person. Open-mindedness and flexibility are contagious qualities. Use them liberally.

THE TOOL

If you catch yourself or someone else fighting a battle with the 'I know what I like and I like what I know' syndrome, here are some reminders for you and them on the benefits of giving a fresh perspective a second thought.

FIGURE 10.1   Embracing a flexible mindset

 Don't lose sight of the goal

 Really listen

 Keep learning

 Value other perspectives
(especially if they're different to yours)

 Embrace something new as exciting, not threatening

 Rediscover the art of conversation

 Have fun

Don't lose sight of the goal

Putting the cause at the centre of your decision making and accepting that your role is to reach that goal, not feed your ego, will make it easier to divorce yourself from questions like 'am I right or wrong' and instead ask 'is this right or wrong for the situation we are faced with'.

Really listen

How much more intoxicating to consider the idea that some combination of wordage might come along that will flip a few neural switches and actually make you feel differently about something.

Keep learning

Try to put some distance between your confirmation bias and lazy stereotypes and consider a situation or facts from a different point of view. Most of us will see the world differently after becoming a parent, coming out the other side of an illness or suffering loss.

Value other perspectives (especially if they're different to yours)

With the average human attention span dwindling below that of a goldfish's at eight seconds (Research by Microsoft Consumer Insights Group, Canada, 2015) it's hard to imagine any of us giving our conversation partners a fair hearing. Most conversations are more stimulating when you actually pay attention to what is being said. Both parties get more out of it. And when you really listen with undivided attention, you'll find that your mind is more open to new ideas.

Embrace something new as exciting, not threatening

If we attach ourselves too much to our own opinions, we fear losing what we have and fail to see what we could gain if we tried a different direction of travel. Loss aversion is a powerful behavioural barrier.

Rediscover the art of conversation

Lastly, don't you miss the days of a good old-fashioned debate where you were forced to deploy facts, eloquence and a healthy amount of persuasive *je ne sais quoi* to get your sparring partner to take on board a different perspective? It's important not just to stake facts, but to contextualise them in a way that makes their impact unignorable.

> Have fun
>
> How dull it is to sit and listen to another human being with a mind shuttered and unreceptive? And how frustrating is to talk to someone whose mind is coated in neurological Teflon?

THE INSPIRATION

Kawal Shoor and Navin Taljera, Founders of The Womb, India.

Kawal and Navin, founders of The Womb, India's most awarded independent advertising agency, have grown up in a society that embraces flexibility more than many others. As Kawal pointed out at the very beginning of our conversation 'we have 33 million gods in India.' Compared to many other cultures with only one god to turn to, India has many more gods and goddesses to engage. But if this is about the past, the future is equally fluid.

Sitting in Europe with admittedly nowhere near enough exposure or appreciation of this South Asian powerhouse, India has long struck us as a society characterized by a can-do and opportunistic dynamic that shows off most western countries as hamstrung and bureaucratic nemeses of flexibility.

> We are an old country, but a young nation. Our average age is 27 years old. Compared to Japan where it's 48 years, and the UK where it's 40 years, India has a very young mentality. When you're 27, you don't have any clear goals yet. You're not set in your views and ways. Everything a 27-year-old does is idea or opportunity based, not objective based. 27-year-olds don't overthink, they're not overcoached. There is no black or white. India lives in the grey.

Kawal and Navin have built successful careers by understanding the nuance in the behavioural and cultural dynamics of their country, how these have shifted and where they are heading.

'There has definitely been a shift in India over the past 20 years. We have become much more confident. Just look at our cricket team. Our captains were once considered diplomatic statesmen. Today we are much more assertive.' India's cricket captain, Virat Kohli, recently refused being called 'the most Australian non-Australian cricketer of all time' by Australian cricket legend Greg Chappell, insisting he represents 'new India'. According to As Kohli says: 'this for me is a representation of the new India where we want to take on challenges and move forward with optimism and positivity and make sure we are up and ready for any challenges that come our way.' (Monga, 2020).

Kawal and Navin point that taking a fluid approach to challenges can be explained by the predetermination of what success looks like.

> In India, the goal is to make money. Success is defined by money. And there are many ways to make money. People adjust. We have to be flexible if this kind of success is a precondition. If plan A doesn't work, you go to plan B. Then plan C. We are very willing to change tack mid-way. And you can see this by how our cities behave on the road. Jumping signals, driving against the traffic, cutting in. And if you ask someone 'what are you doing?' they will answer back 'why aren't you doing it?'

There is a word in Hindi called 'jugaad' which beautifully captures Indians' special relationship with a flexible mindset. According to the Oxford Dictionary it translates to 'a flexible approach to solve a problem, that uses limited resources'. This has no doubt led to an unprecedented boom in innovation and is bringing up a new generation of entrepreneurs whose agenda is to get things done, no matter what.

The author Anna wanted to know how this way of thinking and living has impacted on how Kawal and Navin run a creative agency and work with clients. And they were quick to point out that in this context, one must distinguish between the right kind of flexibility and the wrong kind of flexibility.

> We aren't flexible in our values. For us those are integrity, empathy and imagination. Those stay no matter what. But we can be flexible in our approach or strategy in fulfilling those. For example, we don't pitch because it creates an unequal relationship from the start. But that's just a strategy to live up to our values.

Navid adds:

> When clients look up to you for solutions and trust you for solutions, there is such a thing as bad flexibility. And it happens when you don't have a strong POV. You need to show your courage of conviction. Unless there is a new data point or new information, you can't just change your mind because someone is pushing back. And some clients will push back just to see if you have conviction in what you are proposing. When we present work to clients we say today, based on our thinking, this is our recommendation. Give us another two months and it might change. But today this is what we recommend.
>
> This dynamic between core values and flexibility in approach can be witnessed in how brands are built as well. A brand like Tata, with a core value of trust, is not restricted to a core competency when it comes to products. They are flexible to go where the opportunity takes them. They sell everything from cars to home appliances to life insurance. But their core value never changes.

Conclusion

Changing your mind to reflect a shift in circumstance, new information or a different way of solving an old problem should be embraced as an opportunity to strengthen your position, not as a compromise that weakens your resolve. This is especially true of rebuilding, where challenging yourself to break out of established behaviour and thinking patterns is often the unlock to progress. Embracing flexibility in business and life can, as Kawal and Navid have demonstrated, lead to great success as long as we don't lose sight of what we are trying to achieve.

CHAPTER ELEVEN

In pace lies power

'If I get this done twice as fast, it will count for twice as much' – this is your internal pressure cooker speaking.

On **timing**. Timing is the key to comedy and, as it turns out, to rebuilds. Doing the right thing at the wrong time can backfire badly. This chapter explores the use of pace and change of pace in order to get the outcomes you want.

Myth – Achievements count for more when they are reached at speed.

Truth – Tempo is the secret to success. Know when to slow down, stop and even reverse before proceeding.

Myth

Progress is often measured in speed. It's one of those currencies, like money, that carry a sort of weight about them that makes you want to hurry along and be as fast as you can.

You wrote the presentation in one day instead of three? You're marvellous!

You pushed through the change agenda in three months instead of six months? You genius, you!

You checked out of The Priory sooner than anticipated? Well done!

We take a false sense of security in thinking that speed will gloss over any cracks that already exist or emerge along the way. Because, hey, at least you were fast about it, right?

Being stuck in a perpetual holding pattern for that prized first-mover advantage or fastest finishing time will eventually start to take its toll on our performance, recovery and well-being.

Burnouts, breakdowns and backfires will start to creep in where you were expecting success and glory.

Most of us would accept that you wouldn't run a sprint on a broken leg, but we would expect ourselves to turn a failing company around within the year, or a relationship to mend following a romantic holiday.

It's time we re-examined our relationship with speed and accepted that there are often more effective ways to mend, rebuild and progress that don't involve tripping over yourself in haste.

First though, it's useful to understand why we often default to doing things quickly, especially when under pressure. In Daniel Kahneman's bestseller *Thinking Fast and Slow*, he describes our mind's process through two distinctive systems:

- **System 1** operates fast and instinctively, with little effort or sense of voluntary control. 'This is the brain's fast, automatic, intuitive approach'. For example: 2+2 or angry face = danger.
- **System 2** focuses attention on activities that require more mental computation.

'It's the mind's slower, analytical mode, where reason dominates.' This is usually activated when we do something that does not come naturally and requires some sort of conscious mental exertion (Kahneman, 2011). For example: 456+876 or doing sudoku.

While both systems work in a complementary fashion to one another, one tends to take the lead, depending on the scenario. When we find ourselves in situations of stress or volatility, our natural instinct is to immediately react and charge ahead to address it. We are less prone to slowing down or stopping before proceeding. System 1 really comes into its own here. And it's that quick, instinctive reaction to change that has protected our species and kept us alive since our days as cave-people. Luckily, we now live in an environment where, when faced with change or difficult decisions, our well-being doesn't (always) depend on running or chasing. We can skip a beat and chose the tempo at which we proceed, tapping into the more considered side of our brains without compromising the outcome.

Oscar-winning actor Mathew McConaughey is a great example of someone who, in order to rebuild the kind of career he wanted to have, well... stopped for a bit and tapped into his System 2. In the 2000s, McConaughey had become known as *the* leading man in romantic comedies. But, after becoming a father, he desperately wanted to take on more challenging roles. Alas, Hollywood kept knocking on his door with more romantic comedy scripts, so McConaughey decided that the only way to pivot was to take a two-year break, which he called his 'unbranding phase' in order to be able to attract more varied and alternative roles. Most of us, if put in his shoes, would find it hard to comprehend that you would voluntarily put a handbrake on your successful career to take it to new heights. It was a huge risk, but a move that really prompted a re-think both for Hollywood and McConaughey. But it worked. He went on to win an Oscar for Best Actor in 2014 for his performance in *Dallas Buyers Club*. While all was good in the end, he does recognize that taking that time out was a big risk and worked against all common instincts. 'Trust me, I had the last six months before I got that phone call to come back to work in dramas – I did not know if I was ever going to work in Hollywood again,' he said (McKeever, 2021).

Truth

Knowing how to pace yourself is the secret to many a success and turnaround. Such is the importance of pace in sports like running and cycling, that you even have professional pacers who ensure the athletes meet their exact game plan for the race. The pace setter runs a very specific pace (or pace pattern). This allows the athlete to just follow along and worry less about pacing and focus on their own race. And we've all seen or experienced situations when a pace pattern is not adhered to. Someone runs out of the starting blocks to take pole position, only to have completely exerted themselves by the time they still have over half of a race to go, finishing somewhere close to the bottom. Incidentally, this is a lesson the author Anna learnt many times over as a young and budding swimmer. Not only in racing but also in training. Which is why she chose to never swim first in her practice lane but always second, so she didn't have to keep pace or count of the laps.

Sports is an easy example to make the point around pace because it's such a physical experience. But it's no different in business, with your health and even in relationships. If you run at a situation all guns blazing without a plan, it's only a matter of time before you burn your fingers, burn your bridges or spontaneously combust into a ball of fire. It's not always wrong to go hell for leather, but more often than not it's advisable to check the proverbial petrol in your tank and plan for a few pit stops to ensure you reach your destination successfully.

The pressure of constantly (re)acting fast, especially for those in leadership positions, is something most of us will consider part of the job description, even a virtue and a quality to be selected for. And technology has only accelerated this trend. However, a McKinsey study found in working with top teams that speeding up isn't always the answer. It often makes things more complex, consumes more energy and, in the best case, solves only a part of the challenge (Kopka and Kruyt, 2014).

Conversely, the study discovered when top teams slow down, they eventually go deeper and faster into achieving their objectives. They deal more effectively with increased complexity and challenges and burn less energy doing so.

So, why is it then that leaders – and, let's face it, most of us – are sceptical when asked to adjust our pace? The unlikely answer appears to lie in the fundamentals of physics with two opposing views of the world, and as it turns out, on decision making and leadership: Newtonian and quantum theories.

For those of us whose memory doesn't stretch back quite far enough, newtonian physics are based on the principles of speed, mass and inertia. All concrete and calculable absolutes that fit our world view and structures perfectly. I hear a voice in exactly the same way as you hear it. That colour red looks the same to me as it looks to you. A+B =C.

Quantum physics, on the other hand, sees the world as relative. A place where all possibilities exist at any given time. Time is nonlinear. Light can behave both as a wave and a particle. Your experience of something, a sound or a colour, is not necessarily exactly the same as anyone else's. For leaders this means being cognoscente that our challenges are complex and that we need to pace the speed of our work, slowing down at times for a deeper dialogue and understanding of our challenges and speeding up elsewhere in the process. David Strauss, CEO of Reason Ventures argues: 'Perhaps the most important element of the quantum world view is knowing that solutions are always available and require only that we be conscious enough to see them. If we are, we set the right attention and intention, directing our energy to the solutions we want to emerge.' (Strauss, 2018).

Todays' leadership practices are still largely based on the newtonian way of thinking. They strive to control and structure their challenges to guarantee outcomes and deliver hard KPIs. This is an efficient, mechanistic way of thinking, working and problem solving by moving as fast as possible from A to B in a controlled and straight line. What it leaves less room for, however, is the softer side of leadership which is arguably where most of the magic happens. As Pieter Nota, then-CEO of Philips Personal Health business, put it, 'the soft stuff is what really makes the hard stuff happen.' (Kopka and Kruyt, 2014).

Appreciating the complexity of a situation (without getting paralysed by it) and adopting different speeds or paces to work through it, is a skill that we will have to embrace if we want to create an inclusive, innovative, and commercially successful business environment. The George Floyd murder in 2020 kicked off a debate for many companies around inclusion and diversity that couldn't, and shouldn't have, been solved as efficiently as possible. The process of creating a truly inclusive culture and policies needed, by default, to be led by a diverse group of employees. Not just the C-suite or the HR department. And this required time, patience and a long-term commitment to the ultimate goal.

So what does this mean for rebuilders? What can physics and an understanding of how our brain processes decision making teach us about the pace at which we go about solving life's challenges?

Speed alone often gives a false impression of progress, as it measures change instead of genuine improvement. But our instinct to keep moving is a hard one to override as we've been doing it since we were cave men and women, hardwired to constantly move in unpredictable outdoor environments (Medina, 2008). So it really goes against our human nature to pause, especially when we feel a sense of urgency to leave a bad situation behind us as quickly as possible. But as we have seen, there is a lot to gain by consciously thinking about the pace we adopt. A leisurely trot, a speedy sprint, a long slog taken attacked at a steady speed… each decision will benefit from a different pace at which you solve it.

As long as we aren't trying to escape a situation that is posing a physical threat, feel free to challenge your internal speedometer. Taking your foot off the pedal might save you time, help you make better decisions and facilitate a more enjoyable and fruitful outcome. As a CEO of a global agrichemicals company once shared: 'what time you lose in decision making, you gain in execution' (Chang and Groeneveld, 2018).

THE TOOL

Always consider the long-term consequences of your short-term decisions

The impact of your decision should guide the tempo at which you implement your actions. Pace is not always about being fast or slow. Equally, an impact is not always about something very important or something trivial. A relatively mundane matter may have a huge impact, whereas something that may seem like a big deal is actually trivial in the long-term. That is why it is important to think of the impact of your decision, before you consider the actions you need to take.

This tool is designed to help you categorize your decisions according to their impact. The pace will then help you decide which actions to take as you can see in Figure 11.1.

FIGURE 11.1 Pacing for impact

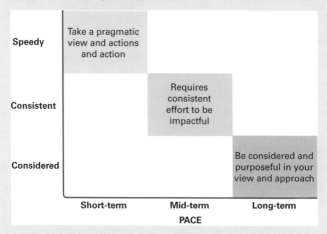

Scenario 1: rewarding staff

Issuing a small pay rise or bonus to someone who has gone above and beyond in delivering for your business. This can easily be written off as a fairly trivial and mundane decision. It might be that you're under pressure to hit your numbers for the year and giving this particular person – let's call them Jay – some extra money might be hard to justify at this time of year.

Default Pace: To get it off your to-do list, you quickly file this as an urgent action for the next financial year.

Actual Impact: The lack of immediate recognition makes Jay feel unappreciated and she decides to start looking for a job elsewhere. Jay is in charge of one of your largest client relationships and they love her and trust her. If Jay goes, this could seriously destabilize their business for your company.

High impact at a considered pace: Given the potential impact of not giving Jay a pay rise this year, it's worth considering this a high impact scenario and spending some time to get to a solution that makes Jay feel appreciated and still enables you to meet your KPIs.

Scenario 2: addressing aches and pains

Your lower back has been causing you problems for months now. You keep putting off a visit to the doctor's because you are too busy. Instead, you treat flareups and symptoms with ibuprofen when they get too bad to ignore.

Default Pace: You address the severity of the pain as and when it occurs. You're simply reacting to your symptoms and do what it takes to make them better as immediately as possible.

Actual Impact: As the months pass, you are finding yourself increasingly distracted by not feeling 100 per cent. It's hard to concentrate sitting down for prolonged periods of time, you can't go to the gym because it hurts your back too much and every which way to move, sit or stand is uncomfortable at best, painful at worst.

High impact at a consistent pace: The impact of feeling physically unwell over a prolonged period of time will eat away at your energy levels, interfere with your well-being and, there is the obvious risk of your health deteriorating.

Your physical and mental well-being requires consistent nurturing. Your body won't benefit from a health spurt, nor can it wait until you've mapped out the course for direction. A steady pace, with consistent attention will do the job.

Scenario 3: naming your band

Naming your band, your business or your offspring can seem like a daunting task that you should dedicate the maximum amount of time and planning to. Afterall, it will stay with you for a long time!

Default Pace: Give yourself as much time as possible. Think it through. Overanalyse it. Put it through research. Sleep on it… a lot.

Actual Impact: There is no question about it. Names are important. But they are important because they represent what you do. The music you make. The people and the personalities in a group. A name is meaningless unless it's attached to something.

Long-term impact at a speedy pace: Dave Grohl, founder of the Foo Fighters famously insisted that a more appropriate band name could have been chosen. 'Had I actually considered this to be a career, I probably would have called it something else, because it's the stupidest…band name in the world.' (Murray, 2010). But because Dave writes great music and is an incredibly likeable character, it really doesn't matter what he calls his band. Therefore a speedy decision-making pace is an entirely appropriate one to adopt, as the long-term impact is dictated by his music and persona, not the name of the band.

THE INSPIRATION

Aline Santos Farhat, Unilever's Chief Brand Officer and Chief Equity, Diversity and Inclusion Officer

Aline Santos Farhat's story starts with *Alien*. Well, Sigourney Weaver actually. When the iconic movie was released in Brazil in the mid-1980s, it went through a rather odd translation process that turned the title 'Aliens' into 'Aline.' An unlikely namesake that our real Aline was teased for at school for being a creature from outer space. When she finally went to the cinema to check out the movie for herself, she was surprised to experience a transformation of her own. Sigourney Weaver's embodiment of a strong and powerful female protagonist was a completely new kind of female role model that Aline hadn't come across in her family circle, where women were mostly stay-at-home mothers or teachers. A hard-nosed warrior woman became a whole different benchmark for a young girl growing up in a patriarchal society. And so, it was to mark the beginning of Aline's life as an activist. First creating a lingerie business at university, which she was eventually forced to put on hold due to popular demand. Then joining Unilever as a graduate to gain more experience in marketing to apply to her lingerie business further down the line. But she never left.

Unilever (a multinational consumer goods company which houses brands like Dove, Persil, Axe/Lynx, Knorr, Magnum and Heartbrand (Wall's) ice cream in its portfolio) has become her campaigning ground for what Aline and Unilever call 'unstereotyping'. The Unstereotype initiative, founded in 2016, is Unilever's commitment to eradicate harmful stereotypes from marketing and to advance more unstereotypical, modern and progressive portrayals of people. With Unstereotype Unilever is challenging itself to create marketing, not just advertising, that will help influence the next generation of people to be free from prejudice. Aline's passion for putting things right that are wrong has found the perfect platform in a company that holds itself and its brands to a higher purpose than merely selling deodorant and ice cream. Considering the numerous cultural nuances that come into play across the world, being able to tackle these often-sensitive topics at the right time with the right amount of momentum is where half of the battle is won. Timing is everything, but pace helps you hit those times.

From challenging traditional household gender roles to redefining masculinity, endorsing same sex relationships, and supporting human rights it has been a journey that has challenged the organization as much as its audiences.

We have definitely become better at taking decisions faster and at embracing experimentation and then pivoting if it doesn't work. That wasn't traditionally in our culture. But it is now. When we think about innovation, we don't think about innovation as an amazing idea that's built in isolation… we think about innovation through real pain points that need solving for consumers. A real problem not a fictional problem. We are continuously challenging ourselves to see if our assumptions are right. We are in the business of finding real solutions for the problems consumers may have. We want to get on the front line and make products that are inclusive, that are innovative and needed in this world.

This process is a lifelong commitment for Aline who has found her sweet spot both at Unilever and the wider marketing community. With the scale and geographical footprint to make a real difference, Aline has become a master at negotiating this change, rebuilding new reference frames across the globe, sensitive to nuance and culture. And it's a balancing act to make sustainable change at the right pace. How does Aline manage to shift and change expectations around harmful gender stereotypes, inclusivity, and people with disabilities in markets with varying experience and acceptance of these topics? She likens it to eating hot porridge.

> You never put your spoon in the middle of the bowl or you'll burn your tongue. Instead, you take your spoon along the border and slowly but surely eat the porridge. It's the same with equity, diversity and inclusion issues. If you want to be a rebel and come into a country and say 'it's absurd you don't accept people with different sexual orientation', that country will smash that rebel and you burn your tongue with hot porridge. You need to be smarter than that. You need to start from the borders but keep challenging slowly. Keep going. Keep going. Keep going. That's why at Unilever we are progressing all the time. We just keep going without burning our tongue but without staying still. That has been very successful for us.

Conclusion

We will always feel the temptation and pressure to be as quick and as efficient as possible, especially when it comes to agendas with a commercial goal at stake. But we mustn't forget the impact we are trying to achieve and the pace that will help deliver it. Or, put differently, the impact we can expect based on the pace we've adopted. Patience and impatience are both valid drivers. Just make sure they serve your ultimate goal.

CHAPTER TWELVE

Finding certainty in uncertain times

'How do I keep my head above water when I can no longer see which way is up?' we ask ourselves in the midst of turmoil.

On uncertainty. To be good at embracing change we must become equally good at spotting what doesn't change. This chapter explores how focusing on what needs to stay the same is the secret to surviving uncertain times.

Myth – When everything changes, change everything.
Truth – Deploying our anchors creates stability when we need it most.

Ever had a day where you feel like you have been put through a mental washing machine? Or perhaps a week, a month or a year like this? Everything keeps changing and as fast as you alter course and replan, things shift again until you can no longer tell up from down or forwards from backwards.

In September 2021, *Harvard Business Review* said:

> Prior to the pandemic, the working world already felt to most of us like it was undergoing rapid, unrelenting change – changes in customer preferences, client and employee expectations, and competitive advantages. Covid-19 managed to upend the few things that felt relatively predictable, like where we spent our working hours, how we collaborated with colleagues, and whether or not we bothered to put on real pants each day. (Grant and Goldhamer, 2021).

When even *Harvard Business Review* is questioning whether or not we need to wear real pants, we are definitely living and working in uncertain times.

Myth

So how should we deal with these levels of uncertainty and the inevitable rebuilding that comes off the back of periods of change? One school of thought is that we should lean in and change everything. Throw it all up in the air and run towards the future. To do anything less is to be a luddite, a stick in the mud, a change denier. In the technology-driven, communications industry where Anna and Sara have spent their careers, this debate regularly rages. Should companies race ahead and embrace the new with wild abandon? Or is this too risky, too unstable, and too likely to see the baby thrown out with the bathwater? Does chasing change leave companies at risk of becoming 'the dog that barks at every passing car'? A wonderfully phrased warning from David Wheldon, former CMO of RBS, who cautioned against mindlessly racing after every new and shiny thing that comes along.

And what about individuals? How can we navigate periods of deep uncertainty and rebuilding when we find ourselves torn between the security and familiarity of what we know, and the desire to embrace the new? How do we find our way through those times when we feel like we don't even know which way is up?

Let's start by exploring why it is that uncertainty discombobulates so many of us. While it is true that different people can find comfort with different levels of change and disruption, in general our brains can only handle so much change at one time.

Psychodynamic counsellor, Amy Walshe, outlines what happens to our brains when we face huge uncertainty. If we aren't sure what's around the corner or what will unfold next, then our brains translate this as a risky situation and go on high alert. She explained to us:

> When we face a big threat, our brains are programmed
> to react to that threat. This is the 'fight, flight or freeze'
> response. We see a saber-toothed tiger coming at us and we
> might run away if it looks too big to fight. Or we might
> simply freeze up and pretend we are dead.

The sympathetic nervous system triggers the fight or flight response, and the parasympathetic nervous system drives the 'freeze' response. We will all recognize the many physical changes that happen in tandem with these neurological responses; heart racing and adrenaline pumping designed to help us fight hard or run fast. In the modern day these responses help us automatically react to many everyday dangers. They make us feel wary when walking in a dark street and slam on the brakes when the car in front stops suddenly. However, this response is less helpful when dealing with the complex threats of the modern world such as emotional turmoil, economic uncertainty and the impact of a global pandemic. During times of huge upheaval in our lives, Amy says that 'our brains perceive ambiguity and uncertainty as a threat in our environment and it can cause people to feel generally anxious. During the Covid-19 pandemic, referrals to the NHS for anxiety have gone up a lot.'

This fearful state promoted by the modern world, makes it difficult to access the clear thinking and clear action we need to resolve complex situations. Figuring out how to handle a difficult redundancy conversation or what steps to take to secure a faltering business or relationship, can't be resolved by simply running up a tree or playing dead. In addition, if we find ourselves in an uncertain position for long periods of time, we can begin to feel exhausted and burnt out, as experienced by many people during the Covid-19 pandemic.

Our brains dislike uncertainty so much, that uncertainty around bad events happening can take more toll on us than the events actually coming to pass. In a research project, the participants told that they had a 50 per cent chance of receiving a painful electric shock experienced more agitation and anxiety than the participants who were told they were definitely going to receive a shock (de Berker et al, 2016).

Worrying about the shock caused more angst than the shock itself. So, when we feel like we are in a mental washing machine and everything around us is being turned upside down, it is no surprise that we find ourselves struggling. Just when we need our wits about us to process and absorb change, we can find ourselves losing our footing altogether.

Truth

Mathematician John Allen Paulos was spot on when he wrote, 'Uncertainty is the only certainty there is. Knowing how to live with insecurity is the only security' (Paulos, 2004). Given that humans aren't naturally wired to cope with vast quantities of uncertainty it is no surprise that whole industries have sprung up to help us fill in the blanks. For eons, cults and fundamentalist religions have promised followers they have special inside knowledge about what will come to pass and remove anxiety from their followers by prescribing rigid and unambiguous rules to live by. In the corporate world there are futurologists (yes that's a real job title), trend forecasters and consultancies who promise to reveal what can be found around the next corner. And the turbulence of recent years has seen a boom in alternative ways of predicting and making sense of events with the growth of tarot, crystals and astrology. Leading astrologer Susan Miller gets over 11 million unique users a month to her website, and new horoscope apps are popping up regularly driving the growth of an industry now estimated at over $2.2bn and growing fast (Kaplan and Stenberg, 2020).

If we don't wish to join a cult or refer to Mercury in retrograde, then there is another method to help navigate uncertainty. While everything being thrown up in the air sends our brains into meltdown, focusing on things that stay the same can help us deal with change. It may seem contradictory, but finding things which remain constant helps us handle change and even helps us to change in tandem with our surroundings. We can think of these constants as anchors in stormy waters. Anchors still allow a ship to rise and fall with the ever-shifting waves but prevent a boat from becoming completely unmoored, getting way off course or crashing on the rocks if seas get very stormy. And if a boat needs to move location completely it doesn't cut the anchor loose. It picks it up and places it down in whatever new place it finds itself to provide security in its new surroundings.

Anchors provide similar benefits in our lives and work. They keep us grounded, providing a sense of consistency and routine. They can help us feel secure when it feels like everything is in turmoil and they help us navigate turbulence by providing touchstones to remind us of who we are and what is important to us. So what can anchors look like in our lives? We may have many personal anchors including everyday rituals and routines like exercise, reading, cooking or speaking to friends and family. Less tangible anchors that are vital in shaping our sense of identity and how we live, include our values, behaviours, ethics and our spiritual or religious beliefs.

Individuals and companies also have professional anchors. As individuals these range from our salary, job title and responsibilities through to our desk, office or friends at work.

In companies, aspects like processes, culture, values, buildings, codes of conduct and even floor plans all anchor a company operating in a particular way.

The great 'work from home' experiment for office workers in 2020 and 2021 is a powerful example of what can happen when too many anchors are severed at once during periods of upheaval. Against a backdrop of huge social and cultural anxiety, many people also found themselves with every aspect of their work routine upended. While there were many positives in terms of increased flexibility and the removal of wasted commute time, this total change of routine also came with downsides. There was no time to oneself during a commute, no face-to-face contact, no dedicated workspace, no chat with colleagues. Without these anchors, normally relied upon to separate work from home and to reduce stress levels, many workers found themselves struggling. Over time some people learned to build in new rhythms and routines to help manage their mental and physical health like carving out a replacement commute time in the morning where they took a short walk to get some air or listen to music before returning to the house to begin work. Or changing out of the clothes they had been working in all day and putting on more casual clothes in the house when their working day ended. Regular contact with people we know is also a critical anchor for many. Those Zoom quizzes and virtual coffees in the early days of lockdown may have been annoying, but they were a natural human attempt to reconnect and anchor back with people we know and were particularly important for those home workers who lost connections with colleagues and friends in the workplace.

To further explore the impact of anchors on people and organizations we looked inside one of the world's fastest moving working environments, the NHS. We spoke to Steve Andrews who is Associate Director for Leadership at East and North Hertfordshire NHS Trust. Steve began his career as a nurse specializing in the care of children and young people with cancer. He progressed to the senior levels of nursing before turning his focus to leadership development and improvement, after realizing how vital it was to help colleague thrive in a constantly shifting healthcare setting. The NHS is one of the largest employers in the world, and continually improving how they work together is an enormous and evolving challenge, subject to the turbulent landscape of politics, funding, and public health crises. In early 2020 the NHS was tackling the UK outbreak of the global Covid-19 pandemic. Steve outlined how almost everything changed for everyone in the organization, even those not directly working on Covid-19 wards.

> We lost control of our time because scheduling totally changed. People temporarily lost control over their roles and jobs because areas like outpatient clinics were closed, and people were reallocated, so they effectively lost their previous jobs. This often happened with pace, and such loss of control generated other losses such as certainty, comfort, competence, team relationships, established leadership etc, all hugely unsettling. Perhaps they were a specialist nurse, but they are now transferred to A&E or they were a non-clinical member of the team now supporting clinical areas. At the same time staff were losing control over things outside of work. Holidays were cancelled, they lost control over

children attending school, over being able to get shopping done. Dealing with loss became recognized as a significant support need.

The NHS is no stranger to disruption and has many organizational and cultural anchors to help the staff and services keep functioning in the face of such widespread uncertainty. Key to this was looking at what made Covid-19 similar to previous crises, not just what made it unique. Rather than looking for only what they didn't know, they looked for what they did know, to help identify where previous experience could be repurposed. This started by asking which of the NHS's existing skillsets and competencies could be connected to the pandemic. Steve notes that the terminology used in the NHS is designed to aid clear identification of familiar situations and responses.

We deployed language and procedures around 'isolation', 'infection control', 'risk', etc. Many of which we are familiar with from other outbreaks such as norovirus. All the time we are drawing on previous experience and skills. Then when we bump into something new, we use a new language to denote that and we ask, 'does the previous skillset we have, meet the need we have in front of us? If not, what's the gap and how do we fill it'. In those early weeks and months, we called upon language which was familiar, processes that were familiar and principles that were familiar to help make sense of the situation.

The principle of the compassionate care, the principle of family involvement, the principle of supporting colleagues, the roles of clinicians. The core principles were in play, but the question was continuously asked again, consciously or unconsciously, about what gaps were merging or what needed to change. What does patient care look like in a Covid-19 world? What does keeping our staff safe look like in that world? What does teamwork look like in that world?

Steve's account highlights some key ways to deal with seemingly wholly new circumstances. This begins with breaking down the situation into component parts to identify what elements of it have been faced before in some form. Then identifying what skills and approaches have worked before similar or analogous situations. This approach is used regularly in high stakes and fast-moving environments like the military and crisis response, but it can be used by all of us to find anchors in uncertain situations. Even if at the outset we feel utterly untethered, we can break down what we are facing into component parts, many of which will start to look familiar, helping us delineate what hasn't changed, from what is truly new. This enables us to draw on existing skills and strengths that we feel confidently have worked for us before in a similar setting. Steve also points out how using familiar language and terminology for the familiar elements can help us feel more confident in dealing with them. While never seen before elements can be highlighted by coining a new term or name. Clearly identifying what stays the same conversely helps the teams tackle what is wholly new. Whether the cause is norovirus, ebola or Covid-19, 'isolation' is a well-understood practice with well-understood protocols.

Outside the NHS a disagreement with our boss or our parents is still a disagreement and the approaches for getting to agreement will be more similar than different. Lastly, Steve calls out the importance of reminding ourselves what principles and values we still hold dear during change. For the incredible staff in the NHS, it is 'the principle of the compassionate care, the principle of family involvement, the principle of supporting colleagues'. Why they go to work never changes, even if what they are doing once they get there is upended.

While the concept of anchors might seem very simple, they play a huge part in our ability to roll with change and adjust to what comes our way. The NHS example is a powerful way of showing how they help within an organizational context but they are equally important within everyday life and often very simple to build in. Steve is also clear on some of the anchors within his own daily life that allow him to work in a sustainable way, supporting others every day. One of these is maintaining a clear period of 45 minutes every morning away from meetings or other people. 'I used to have a 45-minute commute every day but when I moved to a new hospital my commute time became very short. I quickly realized that as an introvert that period of time was important for me so now I get to the office 45 minutes early every day and take that time for myself.' The need for this type of personal stabilization is widely noted by change management experts. Heifetz and Linsky have written multiple books around high stakes leadership and they have this to say about CEOs and top leaders surviving change management programmes. 'To survive the turbulent seas of a change initiative, you need to find ways to stabilize and anchor yourself.' Their examples include: 'Establish a safe harbor where each day you can reflect on the previous day's journey, repair the psychological damage you have incurred, renew your stores of emotional resources and recalibrate your moral compass.' While they are advising top-level executives, the solutions they recommend are remarkably simple and available to everyone. Items like creating a safe haven at a friend's house, at your own kitchen table or during a walk in the woods every day, plus having a confidant outside work that you can share the full 'undigested mess' with without fear of judgement (Heifetz and Linsky, 2014).

We have explored how finding the things that anchor us and create stability during change can help us feel grounded and better able to manage and flex during uncertain times. It is worth noting that they can also help or hinder positive changes taking root. Just like the ship's anchor that we need to take up to move locations, sometimes we need to lift up and even swap out some of our own anchors for real change to occur. Take the example of trying to cut back on alcohol. It can be tricky to achieve if we stick to the same rhythms and routines. If we still hang around the same pub with the same friends and still have curry night on Thursdays, these anchors may keep us rooted in old drinking patterns. If we meet our friend for a walk rather than a pint, head home rather than the pub and replace curry night with movie night, then these new anchors can assist our behaviour change. The same is true at an organizational level. Unchanged anchors are the nemesis of many a change programme and often thwart long-term rebuilding. John Kotter, Professor of Leadership, Emeritus, at the Harvard Business School has spent decades

studying why business transformation does, and more importantly, doesn't work. He has designed an eight-stage model
and the last and final stage is 'anchoring new approaches in
the culture' (Kotter, 2012). He notes that without this critical
final stage, short-term gains will be lost and businesses drift
back to their entrenched, legacy ways of doing things. He
prescribes making adjustments to align an organization's
culture, values and talent to the new way of doing things.
This means looking at new hiring and promotion processes,
examining rewards and incentives programmes and identifying the less tangible norms and values that influence behaviours. These examples are all too familiar in the corporate
world. A company makes a pledge to address the gender
balance in their organization but the hiring process continues
to be the same, there is no menopause policy, the parental
leave policy remains unchanged and the senior male leaders
talk across female colleagues in meetings. Unsurprisingly the
gender balance doesn't improve because despite a new goal,
old anchors remain, and new ones are not built in.

THE TOOL

To identify your own anchors, it is best to begin during a
period of calm. Once the maelstrom hits it can be harder to
see what is working well for us. At its simplest this means
taking an audit and noting down what currently serves you
well. What anchors are fundamental to you, your well-being
and identity? What do you instinctively feel you would want
to keep hold of and what could be exchanged or let go of?
For example, Sara enjoyed having a senior position and title
in an organization and had got used to the reputational

status being a CEO lent her. However, when she began to want more flexibility in her working life, she accepted that she was happy to forgo her senior title and position for the extra freedom that being self-employed would bring her.

The tool below will help you explore anchors across different categories to capture the small daily habits plus the less tangible but crucially important ones like ethics and values.

When change occurs or you are thinking of implementing change, refer to or update this list. Exploring what serves you well and should remain consistent and enduring versus what you are happy to evolve. Do some anchors need to be ejected and let go of completely while some new ones are built in? Are you changing too many at once or holding on to some that it is time to let go of?

EXPLORING ANCHORS

FIGURE 12.1   Tool to explore your anchors and to review them as circumstances change

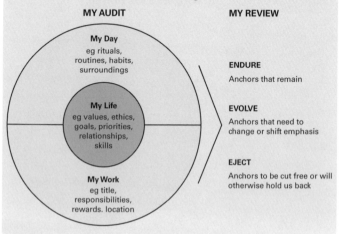

MY AUDIT

My Day
eg rituals, routines, habits, surroundings

My Life
eg values, ethics, goals, priorities, relationships, skills

My Work
eg title, responsibilities, rewards. location

MY REVIEW

ENDURE
Anchors that remain

EVOLVE
Anchors that need to change or shift emphasis

EJECT
Anchors to be cut free or will otherwise hold us back

THE INSPIRATION

Abigail Comber, Chief Marketing Officer, Cignpost Diagnostics, former Chief Marketing Officer, Debenhams

With decades of global marketing experience, Abigail Comber has seen more than her share of turbulence. In her 17 years at British Airways, ash clouds, baggage strikes, a disrupted move to Terminal 5 and a pension crisis were just a sliver of the issues that caused widespread disruption. In 2020 she entered a perfect storm of Covid-19 chaos when she accepted the role of Chief Marketing Officer at the already beleaguered retailer Debenhams, just six weeks before the pandemic hit the UK. She had gone in eyes wide open with a remit to use her exceptional experience to help turn the retailer around by winning back customers. She had just finalised a plan and got buy-in from the top executive team when everything changed.

> We thought that the revenues might wobble, the murmur of something coming across from China, but the rest is history. Six weeks in, I was going to be the person who transforms it all. Eight weeks in, I was going to be the person who worked with them on Zoom and had 120 people reporting into me, trying to keep the business going online when the stores started to close.

Abi's time in that role is a masterclass of how to roll with the punches. She rolled through store closures, store reopenings, a new finance deal that looked like it might save some of the footprint and finally a deal with online retailer BooHoo that didn't avoid store closures but did retain the Debenhams brand. The job changed from week to week. One week, it was to move us to online, and the next week I had to start an entire call centre because our call centre supplier let us down when Covid-19 hit. I was working with IT to get laptops out to 100 people from closed stores that otherwise would have been made redundant and setting up a contact centre for people whose orders may not have arrived.

Speaking to Abi it is clear she has developed some tried and tested ways to keep herself upright at time like these. One way is to focus on what hasn't changed. 'Reframing is something that I do a lot. I think "Okay, so the situation is no longer this. It's this new one." I haven't changed. The world hasn't changed. I still live in the same place, I have still got an income, but the job I now need to do is X. I reframe my capability into the picture that's now in front of me.'

Abi also has a clear personal value around empathy and respect for people which acts as a strong anchor to guide her actions in and out of work. It helps Abi to stay connected to why she does her role, when times are tough, and leads her to prioritize serving others. 'For me, it's always been about the customer. Whatever happens, just know that the customer is the person who ultimately is affected.'

> At British Airways I once had my entire team going down lists of executive club members doing personal callouts to say, 'Look, we know it's been really disrupted. I recognize you're a really regular flyer. What can we do for you?' We need to remember that the outcome for a customer could be devastating in terms of not getting to that meeting, going on that holiday, that connection that they're trying to remake with somebody. At the heart of any journey there's people involved, just people.

The same motivation steered her at Debenhams. 'At Debenhams, one of my contact centre agents was chasing some suits that hadn't been delivered. Those suits were for a wedding, and that wedding had been pulled forward because the father was terminally ill, and they'd been given special permission. There is a human story at the heart of everything.'

This empathy also extends to how Abi herself wants to be treated. After being screamed at by a senior executive at British Airways she decided it was time to leave after 17 years. 'It was entirely unwarranted behaviour. I thought, "I deserve better than this. I certainly deserve a reasonable conversation." It's unnecessary. And it's inappropriate behaviour between two individuals, never mind in a professional workplace.' It was her wakeup call that the culture she worked in had been changing gradually over time and no longer supported a way of treating others which was integral to her. She chose to let go of the job rather than the values that anchor her.

Conclusion

When everything changes, it isn't wise to change everything. Far smarter to explore and identify what hasn't changed and what shouldn't change. These consistent anchors will remind us of who we are and what endures despite everything. When deployed wisely, anchors provide stable and secure foundations from which to embrace new change and evolve and flex as needed. Becoming aware of our anchors is something we can all begin to do so that when we hit rough seas, we know which of them we need to hold onto and which we need to cut loose in case they sink us.

CHAPTER THIRTEEN

Not all success is successful

*'Other people seem more impressed with my success than
I am'* – *not the thing you want to admit to yourself after
giving it your all.*

On defining success. Who hasn't chased a dream that
turned out to be a nightmare? This chapter explores
the different dimensions of success and how to achieve
what's right for you.

Myth – Success is measured by universal benchmarks,
often money and status.

Truth – Success is as individual as you are.

Our relationship to success in a rebuild is fundamental. Many setbacks have been experienced because individuals follow a path that is celebrated or encouraged by those around them, but they themselves give little value to. They feel any doubts they have in their mind would jeopardize their standing if vocalized or acted upon. Some even forfeit their right to dissatisfaction entirely given the profile of their achievements. This holds countless rebuilders back from setting a more sustainable path forward and often ends in breakdowns, breakups and just a general big old mess. But what happens when our successes don't feel successful? What happens when they feel like a failure? Your benchmarks for success need to be considered carefully because they inform how you spend your time and effort, life and happiness. If you don't measure success in terms that are truly important to you, you can't work towards getting there. Nine times out of 10, the problem isn't with what you are or aren't achieving, it's with your goalposts.

Myth

Most of us grow up hoping to achieve success of some kind. It's an intangible force that is hardwired into our systems and that we chase from the moment we are born, even if we don't know it yet. What often spurs us on in this journey is others' reactions to our actions. First come evolutionary successes that range from sitting up and crawling and becoming more independent to pursuing recognition, favouritism, and later on fame and fortune.

Success is an easy way for us to distinguish between people's perceived worth and contribution. To make it more objective, it's often measured in standardized metrics such as money and status, platform and, in more recent years, likes and follows on social media. The thing about this perceived success is that it is inherently competitive and comparative, characterized by binary metrics that don't account for our individual values and goals. You win or you lose. You're a success or you're a failure. It's about having more, being better and getting ahead... of everyone else.

A little observation to illustrate this is the elusive left-hand turn, as observed by Richard Peters, co-founder of Decoded. For people who have flown first class or have heard friends and colleagues talk about flying in first class, that feeling of turning left is part of that superior experience. Precisely because most of the people on the aircraft have to turn right. Now this is just a theory, but the airline companies in the 1990s that flew business class only may have faced their ultimate demise because business class in the absence of economy just isn't as satisfying. We are bred to think something is better if others haven't got it.

Most people would consider Elon Musk to be highly successful. He has companies, money, rockets, and cars. But with that comes a flipside. In a tweet from July 2017, Musk talked about the by-products of success that people don't see and shouldn't envy (Musk, 2017):

Tweet from @EricDiepeveen: Following @elonmusk on Instagram shows an amazing life. I wonder if the ups and down[s] he had made for a more enjoyable life?

@elonmusk replying to @EricDiepeveen: The reality is great highs, terrible lows and unrelenting stress. Don't think people want to hear about the last two.

Would we consider Elon successful on a happiness or health spectrum? Only he will know. But it's not a metric that achievers are usually defined by. At least not in the eyes of their peers.

Another culprit is our obsession with quantitative measures, perpetuated by a system that is fundamentally binary. Peter Drucker, a prominent management theorist, explained it this way: 'You can't manage what you can't measure.' (Drucker, 1954). Business success is measured in revenue, profit and share price. Personal success tends to be measured in income, status and possessions. Often though it's hard to put a KPI on the things we care about most. Cognitive biases and external pressures get in the way of people realizing what they actually want to achieve, regardless of whether it chimes with expectations around them. Putting a value against a measure that falls outside of societal norms, and chasing it, takes a very conscious and deliberate effort, not to mention a willingness to forgo recognition.

A Hindu saying reportedly says: 'Everyone is a genius. But if you judge a fish by its ability to climb a tree, it will live its whole life believing it is stupid.'

The point that is important to make here is that there is nothing flawed, less ambitious or less inspiring about people whose definition of success differs from your own, or from social norms. We need a radical change in metrics that indicate progression by broadening and redefining the term success in order for it to be more meaningful, relevant and accessible. It should be an inclusive concept that everyone can experience, not just a select few.

Truth

What makes you feel successful? Is it gardening? Is it being in control of your time? Is it helping your community? Or winning large research grants?

The ever-wise Denzel Washington reportedly put it beautifully and simply: 'Success? I don't know what that word means. I'm happy. But success, that goes back to what in somebody's eyes success means. For me, success is inner peace. That's a good day for me.'

A study conducted by Cambridge University called 'The meaning of success' sought to understand and redefine what success meant to a group of peer-nominated, accomplished female university employees (Bostock, 2014). The overall outtake was that success needs a radical overhaul in how we define it. And this redefinition is not about lowering standards, but about enhancing them. Specifically, it was found that:

– Ideas about success had not yet caught up with the societal changes that had brought far more women and people from diverse backgrounds into the workplace, increasing the dimensions of how success is defined and experienced.

– The traditional understanding of success had often disadvantaged the women in particular.

– It was notable that the achievements that mattered to participants often had an everyday feel to them, rather than just being showstopping, big-ticket items. There was clear value in the simple daily practice of engaging constructively with colleagues to do work that was of a high standard and on topics that held a real fascination.

What really brings the multi-dimensionality of success to life are what the women of Cambridge has to say:

'Success is measured in many ways – the most important of which is how you feel about yourself.' Linda King, Director of Studies, St Edmund's College.

'I very much support the notion that 'success' has a million definitions.' Joanna Cheffins, Joint Head of the Legal Services Office.

'Be really hungry for success – but be brave enough to know that success can be measured in many different ways.' Nicola Padfield, Reader in Criminal and Penal Justice; Master of Fitzwilliam College.

The determination to align yourself with the things that matter to you most was mirrored in a study by WeSpire which found that Gen-Z (the newest generation to enter the workforce and also called 'Change Generation' due to their passion and desire to make a difference through work) is the first generation to prioritize purpose over salary. What do they do to prep for an application? They read mission statements and values documents to select where they work in a quest for their employers' values to match their own. Ensuring that organizations are set up to deliver to these shifting definitions of success will be key to attracting and retaining the youngest talent of any industry.

So how can we collectively challenge and expand the meaning of success, especially when you're rebuilding? Whether you're running an organization, working in one or looking to recalibrate your personal growth compass, consider what the concept of achievement means to you by considering the following:

Define your values

- What are the beliefs, the ideas and the ideologies that define and motivate you?
- Which of them would you hold on to at any cost, no matter the reward for breaking them?

Set your goals

- What's the impact you want to make on your own life and on the world around you? These can be qualitative and quantitative measures.
- Think long-term, otherwise you'll get hung up on speed bumps, and distracted by the intermittent highs.
- Don't forget that each setback will have afforded you the opportunity to improve your skillsets, network, and experience.

Choose your success metrics

- Success metrics should reflect your values and measure the difference you see and feel.
- Decide to what extent you want to invite outside feedback.
- It's hardest to measure the things we care most about: mental and physical health, relationships, freedom, and fulfilment. Include some qualitative analysis into your definitions of success.

Keep your nose in your lane

– That's to mean, don't get distracted by what others are doing or achieving. Their success isn't your success. What matters is that you feel motivated and satisfied by what's happening and how you're moving forward.

THE TOOL

Defining success

Consider three simple steps to help you reach your personal definition of success. This applies equally to defining success for yourself or on behalf of an organization.

1 Define your core values.
   → honesty, freedom, empathy, hard work, fun, generosity… There will be many, many more.

2 Define your vision of where you want to be in the future. It could be next year or over a longer period of time. Give yourself enough time and space to achieve your goals.
   → goals that relate to you as an individual, your organization or department, your family, your community… It could be one or some of these and many more.

3 Write down what indicators will prove you are on the right track. You can do this before you embark on your journey and update as you go along.
   → consider a mix of benchmarks that will let you know you are on track. Work satisfaction, employee retention, physical and mental health, me time, holidays taken, money set aside. Again, this will be entirely individual to your goals and circumstance. Remember, this is for you to feel you're on track, not for others.

Your vision for the future and the successes to show whether you are achieving them or not will invariably shift as life and work happens. It's important to adapt to the situation around you without feeling like you're compromising on what's important to you.

FIGURE 13.1   Defining your success through your values and vision

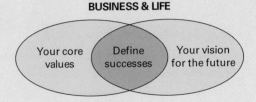

THE INSPIRATION

Cristiana Falcone, Strategic Adviser, Investor, Philanthropist

On sticking to your values, no matter what

When she was born, her name was meant to be Selvaggia (meaning 'wild'). But when the priest advised this wasn't Christian enough, she was, in an ironic act of compliance, named Cristiana. Cristiana grew up in Rome, granddaughter to a strong-willed nonna from Sardinia and the daughter of well-to-do parents. Her upbringing was characterized by strong values that built the foundations for her life's pursuits: finding fulfilment as a human being. Nobility of deeds and actions counted for far more than money made. If every day you could say you were a little bit better than the day before, you were doing well. Above all, freedom and human dignity were the rights worth fighting for; so it is no wonder that Mother Teresa from Macedonia was Cristiana's role model when she was little!

While the life of a nun was not on the cards for Cristiana, she wanted to make a positive impact as a diplomat but, when she didn't pass the exams, she embarked on a bachelor's degree in political science and a master's degree in law and diplomacy. This led her, at the age of 31, to join the World Economic Forum where she long held the position of Senior Adviser to the Executive Chairman and Founder of the World Economic Forum, and is now an independent board director sitting on three boards. But what followed next is something she certainly hadn't planned for as a child or as an independently successful career woman with a strong identity of her own. She met Sir Martin Sorrell, founder and then-CEO of advertising behemoth WPP. He was, and still is, a big personality in his own right, and his world is one that becomes an all-consuming reality for anyone who participated in it. When he proposed to Cristiana after a three-and-a-half-year pursuit, she asked, 'Is this a strategic partnership or hostile takeover?' Assured it was a strategic partnership, she embarked on her next chapter as Lady Sorrell. Being married to a professional powerhouse when you are one yourself is no small feat. Used to self-determining her own courses of action, Cristiana found herself flung into a reality where her life was increasingly defined by her marriage. Carrying the second identity of her husband started to impact on how she could work and live out her personal values. Support was more readily offered for spousal appearances than for her professional pursuits. And this trade-off, she says, was in no small part facilitated by a cultural system that was attuned to prioritizing one partner's success over the other's. In Cristiana's case, her husband's agenda superseded her own. 'You can't work if you're unhappy at home. Your own life comes first. Your personal values should dictate everything, and if what you're doing is at odds with that, you should leave.'

Despite her marriage ultimately coming to an end, Cristiana is succeeding. 'Success is not a linear mindset. To get from A to B you don't have to do it in order. I ask myself, am I reaching my goals regardless of the path I'm taking?'

While Cristiana's view of success was ingrained in her from an early age, and has served as a compass throughout her life, Marc learnt how to define success through being successful but not feeling it. His story is one of discovery, purpose and total commitment.

Marc Lewis, Founder of the School of Communication Arts
On finding your telos

We first interviewed Marc in June 2020 for The Rebuilders podcast. Marc is the larger than life, quirky and brilliantly sharp Dean of the School of Communication Arts, the world's most awarded ad school. With so many accolades to his name, we wanted to know what success, in its broadest sense, means to him.

Success changes your values. If you'd ask me that question 15 years ago, it might have been about bank balance, or it might have been about visits or eyeballs or something like that – it would have been something different, I think. But I think that that is common. Back then I guess I was probably in my late maybe 20s, and now I'm in my late mid-40s. And I think that we have different ways of measuring success.

So what was his first experience of success?

When I sold my first dot com, for about a minute I was a tabloid celebrity, because a 20-year-old selling dot coms were sort of, you know, Sun/Mirror/Star fodder. Then I was running a technology business that had a bunch of IP that was really interesting. And I was getting a lot of interest from a lot of really exciting technology partners and specifically Motorola. And I really wanted to sell to Motorola, and Motorola really wanted to buy. And my shareholders wouldn't let me sell. And I realized I wasn't in control of my own destiny. And I realized what's controlling my destiny is money. Other people's money. So that realization took a lot out of me and I had a breakdown. I disappeared to my in-laws' farm for a year, fed chickens, and had time to think.

What then came of this self-imposed time-out?

I don't know how long I'm on this planet for, but every day I'm going to do it to serve the things that I enjoy. There's a Greek word called 'telos', and the word 'telos' literally means purpose. So I needed to explore what my purpose is. And my purpose is not to make other people money. So that was a huge revelation, and a huge part of my putting myself back together, was understanding what my telos is. And then working out how I play to that telos.

What I was most proud of all the way through my dot com years was everybody that I hired – I hired very young, either straight out of uni or school, or whatever, first-jobbers – very many of them then went onto start up their own businesses, run their own businesses, lead big businesses. So I'm very good at spotting and developing talent. And particularly the spotting bit.

That is when Marc decided that fostering and growing young talent would become his full time calling.

I was a scholarship student at place called the School of Communication Arts in '93, '94, and the School of Communication Arts was a brilliant school run by an incredible man called John Gillard. John had Parkinson's when he opened the school, he retired as I left, and he sadly passed away six years later. And when he retired, the school closed, because the industry was supporting this incredible visionary, rather than a vision. I took the decision in '08 when I came out of my breakdown and came out of the farm to ask the permission of my former classmates Sir John Hegarty, John Gillard's widow, Rosalind, and a few other people for permission to reopen John's school.

I wanted there to be very many more scholarships. And one in three of our students have received a scholarship. And I'm absolutely confident that one of the reasons why we're the very best school in the world, is because of that reciprocity, and the diversity that that spirit of reciprocity allows us to play out.

So having lived through different phases success, what does it mean today?

I think for me, now, success is going to bed at night feeling that everything that you wanted to do that day to try and make that day a little bit better, for either you or the communities around you, that you ticked off a good number of the things on the list that take you closer towards your goals.

And everyone's different right? So they can choose their own frameworks or KPIs or whatever nonsense you want to use to discuss how you measure success. But simply for me, it's like I go to bed at night, and if I'm able to think about how I helped a student, or how I was able to get money out of agencies to fund a scholarship, or you know, if I'm able to think about things that I was able to do in order to try and make my world a better place, it was a success.

Conclusion

If ever you find yourself in a situation where you are achieving, but not feeling like you are succeeding, ask yourself whether your definition of success is designed to make you happy, or whether it's to please the ideals of others. By aligning your core values with where you want to be in the future, you will discover that only you can define success for yourself.

CHAPTER FOURTEEN

Let's all get uncomfortable together

'I don't want to make a bad situation worse so I'll keep my head down and my thoughts to myself' – think many of us when faced with a difficult conversation.

On honesty – move over 'gloss over'. When it comes to rebuilding teams and relationships, it's important to purge any lingering resentments or issues. This chapter explores why and how this can be achieved.

Myth – Let sleeping dogs lie.
Truth – Wake up the dogs: only then do you know what you're dealing with.

The subject of communication, or lack thereof, could have filled an entire book. The failure to communicate has started wars, ended romances and inspired a lifetime of sad songs. Anyone who isn't a hermit will understand that communication is at the very heart of human relationships. It sits at the core of how people do or don't get along and, importantly for rebuilders, it is the foundation for understanding and overcoming challenges. Even though it can be uncomfortable, learning to communicate well means being able to have the hard conversations, tell the tough truths and have disagreements.

Myth

As a Brit, Sara has grown up in a culture that makes not saying things a national pastime. Geoffrey Chaucer was writing about letting sleeping dogs lie back in the 1300s. 'Children should be seen and not heard', 'If you haven't got anything nice to say then don't say anything at all' used to be common parenting phrases. It doesn't make for a natural inclination towards honesty and transparency. In contrast, Anna's German and American background has resulted in a more direct and forthright approach to speaking up, which benefits their working partnership. While Sara is tip toeing around trying to find a polite way to phrase feedback, Anna just comes straight out with it, saving a lot of time in the process.

At first glance the term 'conflict avoidance' might sound like a good thing. Who actually wants to have a conflict? Why would we not want to avoid them? However, therapists and experts in conflict resolution call out conflict avoidance as something to be avoided. Oh the irony. Rather than seek to understand and explore the issue at hand, conflict avoidance just sweeps problems under the carpet to pop out another day like a particularly unwanted dust-bunny. We might also believe that stepping back from conflict is the kind and generous thing to do but the opposite is often true. Experts in managing conflict point out that the 'avoidance' style of conflict management often indicates a low concern for self and a low concern for others (Rahim, 2010). This can feel very counterintuitive but on reflection it makes a lot of sense. If we are unwilling to go through the discomfort of a difficult conversation it actually means we are avoiding doing the right thing for both ourselves and those around us. We are avoiding the opportunity to improve the situation or the relationship by speaking up, and choosing instead to bury our heads in the sand.

The other side of the conflict avoidance coin is being assertive. If you hear someone described as assertive, what do you think? A bit bossy, a bit pushy, a bit out for themselves. In fact practitioners in the area of non-violent communication actually recommend assertive communication as a productive style. Being assertive means 'individuals clearly state their opinions and feelings, and firmly advocate for their rights and needs without violating the rights of others. These individuals value themselves, their time, and their emotional, spiritual, and physical needs and are strong advocates for themselves while being very respectful of the rights of others.' (UK Violence Intervention and Prevention Centre). So much for Sara's approach of politely tiptoeing around an issue. Much better to speak what is on your mind and recognize this as a mark of valuing yourself and others.

It is important to note that the 'respectful tone and regard for others' is a key feature here. It's not just what we say but how we say it that will help resolve issues. Tipping into an aggressive style is to be avoided and can be destructive. Similarly, thoughtlessly blurting out criticism or difficult truths at the wrong moment and without regard for how they will land is not good communication. We have all met the people who say 'I'm just someone who likes to speak my mind' then goes on to be plain rude. Don't be that person. Good communication is about feeling secure enough to speak our honest opinions and advocate for ourselves while respecting the other party. It is a two-way street.

So, the experts tell us that avoidance is bad, and directness is good. But what does this look like in the context of real relationships? And if it can be tricky between two people then what does good look like amongst groups of people? Communicating and resolving challenges between multiple people is even more complex, which is why families make such a good focus for sitcoms. Multiple, interlocking relationships offer infinite opportunities for people to get the wrong end of the stick to hilarious or disastrous effect.

Teams are a similarly rich place to explore what good communication looks like within groups. In many ways they are our 'work families'. A collection of people who spend many hours a day physically or virtually together, with multiple layers of connections. There are formal structures such as reporting lines, plus the informal structures of who does and doesn't get along. Team members may share some common traits, goals and objectives but they will also bring important differences, diverse experiences and personal and cultural viewpoints. What can possibly go wrong! If you have worked in an office or even simply watched *The Office*, then you will have a good idea.

In work as in life, good communication and strong relationships within a team don't mean not arguing or disagreeing. Quite the opposite. If members of a team never speak up to voice a difference of opinion, it isn't a good sign. Harvard business Professor Amy Edmondson of Harvard Business School has spent a career studying what makes high performing teams and successful organizations and points to a vital component called 'psychological safety'. She defines this as 'a shared belief that the team is safe for interpersonal risk-taking.' (Edmondson, 2018). In layman's terms a psychologically safe work environment is one where employees are free to speak up, disagree and make mistakes without fear of being judged, humiliated or punished. If someone feels safe and secure in their role, knowing they won't be judged for speaking their mind then they feel free to disagree, to ask questions and to raise issues. They feel free to try new things, make mistakes and be honest if something hasn't gone to plan. If they don't feel this level of security then they will keep schtum, keep their head down and nod along in agreement. Amy believes that psychological safety is a key ingredient for businesses and teams to be able to improve, innovate and progress. People need to feel free to speak honestly and venture new thoughts and ideas if any innovation and problem solving is to occur. The characteristics of a team that feels psychologically safe include being candid, giving feedback and suggesting improvements plus healthy and constructive disagreements and debates. What this looks like in practice is a lot like being assertive, honest and not avoiding conflict.

By contrast a team that is always polite and never disagrees probably isn't speaking their mind and possibly doesn't feel free to do so without reprisal or repercussions. On a day-to-day basis this robs the team of the ability to learn from each other and to solve issues together but it can also have more serious implications. Frustrations and issues between team members that should be raised get brushed under the carpet and can fester if left unresolved. It also prevents small problems getting raised early which would stop them mutating into bigger problems and sometimes into full-blown, toxic business disasters. If you look back at any large corporate scandal or cover up from Enron to Theranos, it is likely that there wasn't a great deal of psychological safety! In many instances staff will say they felt unsafe and unable to voice concerns before the issues scaled up to catastrophic proportions. Eventually whistleblowers come forward to speak out, often in secret.

A notable recent example is the self-styled punk brewer BrewDog. After years of presenting itself as a plucky, upstart brand on the side of the little guy against the brewing establishment, it recently received a big blow when around 250 former staff penned an open letter to its founders. The staff criticized the culture and atmosphere at the brewer since its inception, citing a toxic and belittling work environment rife with 'lies, hypocrisy and deceit'. The staff claim to have felt powerless to bring concerns to the founder as 'no matter how these were raised, the likelihood was we would be met with some variation on "that's just the way things are". Being treated like a human being was sadly not always a given for those working at BrewDog.' (Punks with

Purpose, 2021). While the founders strive to revive the brand's reputation, this is a cautionary tale of what happens in a business when staff don't feel psychologically safe. A culture of silence and fear evolves with no opportunity to address concerns until an anonymous takedown is posted online.

Truth

If BrewDog is the cautionary tale, how do we avoid it? To understand more about how to keep teams on the right track and how to rebuild if things go awry, we spoke to businesswoman, entrepreneur and author Sophie Devonshire. Formerly CEO at The Caffeine Partnership, one of the UK's leading management consultancies, she is currently Global CEO at The Marketing Society, a global community of leading marketers from the world's best brands including TikTok, Unilever and Amazon. In her many years of working with clients across hugely varied organizations she has helped to build and rebuild many teams to get them working at peak performance. She has spent a lot of time thinking about what makes a team a 'super team' and in doing so she has learned to spot the signs when teams aren't communicating or working well together. Sophie observes that when teams aren't working well it is often tempting to blame the individuals on a team but more often it is how the team is interacting together that is the root cause.

> It often starts with people feeling like things are going too slow. And when you dig deep, and explore what's happening

in the team, there are three big warning signs. There's a lack of candour, a lack of conversational turn-taking and a lack of communication. When I go in and work with these teams you notice a lot of side conversations going on. You spend time with the individuals and they tell you what they are not telling each other because there isn't the psychological safety in the team to do so. There isn't a culture of candour where people are encouraged to discuss things and that is a big warning sign that things aren't working. Regarding conversational turn-taking, the science shows that really strong teams have shared airtime. We have all seen the situation where there is a really strong, dominant leader who does all the speaking in a meeting and then the really smart ones, the introverted ones, or the ones who have great ideas aren't encouraged to speak up and that's another strong warning sign.

She also notes that a lack of clear communication around meetings can often be observed if a team isn't functioning well.

You hear: 'Why wasn't I told about that?' or, 'have you had a side conversation while you're playing golf together?' And there aren't the mechanisms or the culture set up for people to communicate as a team. So those things are really helpful to sense check against. Do we have a culture of candour where people speak up? Do they feel psychologically safe enough to argue with each other? In sessions when we're together does everybody properly have a voice? And in sessions when we're not together how are people learning together, listening together, discussing things together? Particularly, as we're all working in a remote distributed virtual situation which can exacerbate issues. You can't just grab somebody in the kitchen when you're having a cup of tea. So having good communication habits is very important.

So what practical steps can we take to encourage openness and honesty in the teams and relationships that we are part of? The first step is to reframe how we think about speaking up. We should keep in mind that speaking up is an essential step to help any situation or relationship evolve and that holding our tongue isn't the best thing to do. Kim Scott who has written excellently and extensively on this subject in her book *Radical Candour* encourages us to realize that 'truth can accelerate' (Scott, 2017). It accelerates learning, harmony and even rebuilding if things have hit a bump in the road.

The second step is to introduce some techniques that help encourage honesty and candour. It is tempting to think that relationships only reach this level of openness once they have bedded in for some time but there are many tips and tricks to encourage it from the outset.

Sophie has developed her own ways of bringing candour to teams. After meetings she encourages the team to all share their responses to two simple questions. What worked well? And what would be even better if...? This simple approach to calling out something good and something that can be improved sets the tone for new teams to regularly share and improve together. When authors Anna and Sara were running TBWA, the management team used an alternative approach. To ensure that staff didn't hold back from sharing their thoughts, the management team introduced an anonymous way of giving feedback called Pulse. Staff were prompted every Friday to respond by text if they had a good week or bad week and to leave an open comment. Every Monday at 9 am the leadership team would share the anonymous feedback with the company plus how they intended to address any issues raised. It provided a regularly rhythm for sharing the good, bad and the ugly and created a vital feedback loop to build the culture in a transparent way.

There are many other examples out there of companies creating their own tools and techniques to encourage open communications including Airbnb, one of the world's most successful modern brands. Joe Gebbia, who co-founded the business in 2008, wanted to ensure that their culture continued to thrive as it grew rapidly. He introduced the concept of elephants, dead fish and vomit (Gallagher, 2017). These three things provided a way for Airbnb folks to share their thoughts. Elephants were the big things in the room that people weren't mentioning. Dead fish are the past events or decisions that people can't get over. Vomit was for when staff simply needed someone to listen to get something off their chest. As well as creating an environment of candour, giving a name to these three areas also provided language that helped staff name these issues. As well a touch of humour. 'I can smell a dead fish in here folks' is a lighthearted and quick shortcut to drawing attention to an issue long before it becomes serious. Finding a tool to encourage this form of regular sharing in your team, family or friendship group is a great way of creating the good communication habits that Sophie advises. Devise your own language, structure and regular moments in which to use it. As long as it is carried out in a respectful manner it will be a gold mine of valuable insight.

THE TOOL

This tool is a simple but effective one to create comfort around sharing our thoughts in a transparent way. It works equally well in both a professional and personal setting. We have met people who use it nightly around the family dinner table to encourage sharing between reluctant teens and their parents.

The tool is called 'rose, bud, thorn' and Sara was first introduced to it in a professional setting by Sharon Callahan, then-CEO of TBWA\WorldHealth. It was a large post-work dinner with around 25 people, most of whom Sara had never met. The plan was to get to know each other a little before a full day of collaborative meetings the following day. She felt tired and didn't have a huge amount of energy left to engage in small talk. Until something quite unexpected happened. After the meal Sharon suggested they do a round of 'rose, bud, thorn' and While Sharon colleagues were clearly familiar with this practice, Sara had no idea what was coming. Sharon asked each person in turn to speak to the following. A 'rose' was something they felt good about or that was going particularly well. A 'bud' was something they felt had potential and that they felt excited about seeing it unfold. A 'thorn' was something causing concern or presenting a challenge. Sharon went first to set the tone and the team proceeded to share in the most remarkably candid way. The 'thorn' for two senior team members was concern for a fellow TBWA/WorldHealth colleague who was suffering with a serious health condition. They spoke openly, not hiding their emotions or deep worry for this dear friend and colleague. Within 20 minutes Sara went from sitting with a table of strangers to feeling the beginnings of a bond and honoured that they had shared their inner thoughts and shown such vulnerability.

TABLE 14.1 Rose, bud, thorn conversation starter

	Rose – Success	Bud – Potential	Thom – Challenge
General team sharing	What is a highlight at the moment? What is making you feel fulfilled? What are you most proud of?	What are you looking forward to? What are you keen to do more of or learn more about?	What is proving difficult? What are the barriers you are facing? What is the source of the worry?
Actively seeking feedback on a current project	What is currently going well? Where are we having success? What has been effectively completed?	What is going well that we can dial up going forwards? What new ideas do we have that we can try?	Where are we lagging behind? What roadblocks do we need to solve? Where do we need to ask for support?

This simple structure of 'rose, bud, thorn' can be used in limitless ways. You could use it, as above, to set an open and honest tone at the start of a relationship or when establishing a new team, encouraging openness from the outset. It can also be used in a more reflective way to actively seek feedback or suggestions for improvement on a particular topic such as the way a project is being run or how a team is working together. The table below lays out two examples – one example to stimulate general candour amongst a team, the other, to request feedback on a specific project.

THE INSPIRATION

Dr John Curran, Organizational Anthropologist, Executive Coach and Trainer

Dr John Curran is an organizational anthropologist, executive Coach and trainer who works with clients worldwide to address cultural challenges and resolve conflicts. He shared some hugely insightful perspectives on the need to face conflict both personally and professionally and the damage that can be done if we fail to do so. Interestingly he encourages us to accept that conflict is everywhere and that we need to learn to work with it rather than brush it under the carpet.

Conflict is everywhere. It isn't something that happens when things go wrong. It exists around us all the time, the key is to learn how to manage it. With conflict within organizations, conflict should be seen as a natural part of culture and as a form of communication. It's trying to tell you something. What we do though is we either fight it or we run away from conflict.

He regularly sees the impact of ignoring conflict when it starts to leak out in other ways and affect people's behaviour. 'People start performing in different ways. They set up new types of rituals of rebellion, as I call them, instead of having that psychologically safe space where they feel safe to be able to challenge.' These rituals of rebellion can be seen regularly in business if we look for them. People's engagement with work may change, becoming evidently demotivated or frustrated. They may start to exert their agency in another way, maybe not speaking in meetings, disengaging from team sessions, showing up late or not following agreed actions. Critically, all these behaviours are forms of communication if we choose to notice them! If someone is behaving in this way, we should ask ourselves why. Why are they not being listened to and what is gnawing at them?

When working with teams to resolve conflict John outlines the steps he takes. Firstly, the team must identify and own the issues themselves. 'That's not me coming and saying, "There's a problem with you guys." They need to define what is really going on and try and own it.' Secondly, he works to create a psychologically safe environment where people feel free to speak their minds. As a trained mediator and facilitator he creates very clear structure with rules and boundaries that the whole team agrees to. This is the same approach taken by relationship counsellors who create a space with clear rules of engagement so that issues can be safely explored. Lastly, he brings other versions of the truth into the room. As well as large staff surveys to get a 'bird's-eye view' he likes to get a 'worm's-eye view' where he will interview 30–40 staff and share their comments directly with the senior management. 'I feed back as a mirror going, "This is what you said" and then they have to face up to that. Often then, the tension, the conflict begins but it's done in a safe space, because I'm facilitating it.'

John highlights that the need to honestly explore issues and seek resolution is also vitally important in our personal lives. If we don't deal with them directly then we may find out that they leak out or affect our behaviour and in unforeseen ways. This was brought home quite abruptly to him in his own life when he had a heart attack at 47. It hit him like a thunderbolt and kickstarted some healthier lifestyle changes like running regularly and losing weight. What he wasn't expecting were the less physical changes that it precipitated. 'It came as an existential shock to me and my family. It came as a messenger, saying, "You have to deal with certain cans of worms that you haven't opened that exist from when you were a teenager."' Five days in hospital prompted John to explore some challenges that he had kept buried since childhood, stemming from his struggle with undiagnosed dyslexia. Having failed most of his exams, he left school to work as a cleaner in a day centre for the homeless.

> The fact that my dyslexia was undiagnosed meant I had to learn how to perform. In fact, I was doing a lot of the performances that I see in teams today. The performance of being able to be liked, to be wanted and to fit in. I need to make sure that I can move between groups of social networks and be admired, be respected, because I couldn't write, I couldn't read, I couldn't do all that. I developed a big personality instead and was known as 'Big John. [When the heart attack came] it opened up a massive can called 'anxiety'. I'm not saying it was due to being dyslexic, but I know that my dyslexia made me perform and cope and manage my life and play games every bloody day so I could be accepted. My life became very anxiously driven.

Recognizing the anxiety and its root cause didn't resolve it overnight but it allowed him to acknowledge the impact on himself and his family and create a language and tools around managing it. By finally acknowledging his own 'sleeping dogs' it helped it move past them.

It has also led him to double down on his efforts to get teams to open up. He said it has made him a 'a little bit more hard-nosed to get the team moving, to shift them. Instead of thinking "this is as far as I can take you" I will spend even more time exploring ways of opening them up'.

His advice for everyone is rather than avoid the difficult issues 'try to see conflict as a form of communication. It's trying to tell you something. If you can't listen to it, then it's going to get more and more angry that you're not listening to it'.

Conclusion

Having difficult conversations and disagreements can be tough but it gets easier with practice. Getting ourselves into the habit of calmly speaking our minds and getting things out in the open is the most productive way to resolve issues and move past them. It might involve some pain in the short-term but it will avoid more dysfunction in the long run.

CHAPTER FIFTEEN

Making your catastrophe your calling (card)

'I'd like to press "delete" on this experience so nobody will ever know it happened' – what we think when we're in the thick of a catastrophe.

On rethinking your catastrophe. If something goes wrong, we are usually relieved when nobody has noticed or witnessed our faux pas. This chapter explores the benefits of 'unhiding' our personal and professional missteps and shouting them from the rooftops instead.

Myth – Lock your disaster in a safe and throw away the key.
Truth – Bad experiences are just as powerful to own as positive ones.

Catastrophes. Failures. Disappointments. Mistakes. Disasters. Missteps. There are many words to describe experiences that don't go to plan or don't have the outcome we all hoped for. Many of which too rude to mention here! Typically characterized as negative and undesirable, it's no wonder we don't exactly drop them into our social feed or conversation or put them on our cover letters. Which is odd when you consider that failures happen to most of us with intermittent frequency. And they often make for better leanings and stories than successes do. So this is all about reframing a catastrophe, big or small, and making it part of your story and your resilience in positive way.

Myth

Schools, workplaces, inspirational quotes on Instagram: everyone likes to pay lip service to failure. It's part of success, right? It's what happens when you push yourself outside of your comfort zone, right? But when you're in the middle of committing a massive booboo or are staring into the abyss of a spectacular mishap, you quickly realize that, actually, failure is still a pretty bitter pill to swallow. Because the people around us worship success more.

You need look no further than your Facebook, LinkedIn or Instagram feed to see that we are happy to share successes, but most of us steer clear of posting mistakes, much less catastrophes. Smiling kids, beautiful food, promotions, graduations, awards won and holidays taken. All manifestations of what we like to call success. Things that give us bragging rights, status and that oh so smug feeling.

What we don't share as much or at all are our life's outtakes. These we relegate to the pile of 'What was I thinking' or 'Thank God nobody knows'. Unsurprisingly, nobody has invented a platform to share and celebrate this parallel universe on.

There's a reason why Forbes hasn't come out with a '30 people who failed before 30' list. We never talk about the runner up and parents certainly wouldn't entertain a bumper sticker that says 'my child failed their A-levels'.

Funny that, as lowlights certainly out weigh the highlights that make the public cut. Messing up a presentation, failing a driver's test, even a stint in rehab are often more memorable and more human in creating connections with our real and virtual friends. The raw and real reality of something that's gone wrong holds greater emotional pull than the glossy filters we drag our highlights through.

At the centre of this selective-sharing lies our systemic attitude towards failure and our perceptions about the impact a disaster, big or small, will have on our image or future. Sure, we pay lip service to mistakes, but the fact we still feel guarded and uncomfortable around them shows we haven't yet truly embraced their opportunity. Our tendency to share our destination over the journey means we don't really show the workings out in the margins of our life. But it's precisely these workings out that often hold the power, the wisdom and even inspiration for ourselves and others and may just be your key to future success and salvation.

Truth

Being honest is powerful in the best of times. But it's positively contagious in the worst of times. It's seldom we encounter people who willingly and proudly declare an insecurity, worry, wrong-doing or massive mess up.

The power of displaying imperfections was demonstrated powerfully by the 'pratfall effect'. In 1966, social psychologist Elliot Aronson published the effect of a 'pratfall' on increasing likeability after making a mistake. What the study found was that people thought to be competent who then go on to make some kind of blunder are considered more likable as a result, because those blunders make that person more human and relatable. One experiment was an actor delivering a word-perfect pitch to one group, and, in the second group, delivering the same pitch but then going on to spill coffee all over his papers. Far from annihilating his successful performance, the clumsy coffee incident made him go up in the esteem of his audience (Aronson, Willerman and Floyd, 1966).

Clemmie Telford started a blog about challenging motherhood experiences because most of the online forums on mummies and babies painted a rose-tinted picture of an experience that many live as a lonely, self-conscious and frightening time. In her blog, Mother of All Lists, her honesty, and that of her contributors, about early motherhood and raising three kids have turned her into a household name and influencer in this space, before it became cool to share the bad and the ugly. Being open about her darkest days and actively encouraging conversation around them have made her more appealing, more relatable, and ultimately created a successful path in a new direction.

Equal success was found by Herzon Brown, who fell into a life of gangs and crime after suffering an accident that left him scarred and the victim of bullying in his early school years. The sense of camaraderie and family he found in gang life made him feel like he belonged. He decided to break free from gang life after he was nearly stabbed and became a father. Instead of burying his history of crime and adversity, he owned it wholeheartedly and turned it into a career choice.

> I work now as a youth worker and a motivational speaker, deterring others from joining gangs or turning to violence. By sharing my lived experience and the things I've been through, young people can relate to me. I tell them about my life, I show them the scars and they can see their life heading in the same direction. But then they can also see where I am now (Brown, 2022).

It's not in our natural instinct to embrace something that makes us feel bad or negative. It's psychologically hard to view a bad experience as something positive. However, according to self-development author Brian Tracey, taking responsibility for your actions or reactions to a situation automatically short circuits any feeling of negativity you may be experiencing, as it's impossible feel responsible and negative at the same time.

So if we can overcome our negative feelings to a challenging situation by accepting that we take responsibility and exert our power to change how we feel, then we can move towards a space where our catastrophe isn't a ball and chain or a black mark, but a badge of honour and calling card.

Aristotle once observed in his book Nichomachean Ethics (Book 2): 'Again, it is possible to fail in many ways, while to succeed is possible only in one way. For men are good in but one way, but bad in many.'

Putting the classification of good and bad to one side, he makes a good point about failure versus success. In an age where rather than fit in we seek to stand out, disrupt, and challenge the status quo, isn't it much more compelling to do so through an imperfect story? It's certainly much more likely to be unique and punch through the noise of a perfect veneer.

THE TOOL

Extracting positive outcomes

This tool is designed to help you extract valuable experiences out of a situation that would otherwise be classified as a disaster. Sometimes, you'll just want to throw the whole thing away. And there will instances where all the polishing in the world won't get you a piece of gold. Equally, there will be situations that seem bad at first, but with a little distance and analysis, and become something good for you and those around you.

The Act

SOMETHING YOU INSTINCTIVELY CLASSIFY AS A BAD EXPERIENCE, FAILURE, DISASTER

- What happened?
- What was your role, passive or active?
- What do you take responsibility for (could be actions that contributed to the situation or your reaction to something you had nothing to do with)?

The Fact

HOW THIS EXPERIENCE COULD BENEFIT YOU OR OTHERS

- What components should you let go of?
- Which ones are useful to further explore?
- What is useful to share?

The Pact

INSTEAD OF HOLDING THIS AGAINST YOURSELF, OR LETTING OTHERS DO SO, IDENTIFY HOW THIS CAN HELP DEFINE YOUR BUSINESS, CULTURE, PERSONA

- Create a value proposition for your experience.
- Define the key components that are helpful to yourself and others.
- Actively apply and share in all relevant situations.

THE INSPIRATION

Chris Atkins, British Journalist and Filmmaker, author of *A Bit of a Stretch*

We interviewed Chris for our podcast The Rebuilders back in the summer of 2020. Chris had recently published his first book, detailing his experience of going to prison, the British prison system, and what he learnt from the whole ordeal. Naturally, we had so many questions!

'Everything kind of happened for a reason and kicked something really positive off that wouldn't have otherwise happened. My only regret is I wasn't a proper dad in my son's life for 30 months.' The obvious first question for Chris was, what happened?

> The problem with films like mine is that they're very difficult to get funding for. If you've got a nice film about bunny rabbits, then it's very easy to get funding. But if you make films to criticize the government or large institutions, people get quite scared of that.

At the time I was trying to get a film funded there was a culture in the British film industry whereby tax avoidance money was being used to fund movies. Any film made between 2000 and 2010 would have used some tax money in it somewhere. And the basic idea was that rich people, often footballers and city bankers who had been paid far too much money and didn't want to pay any tax, would sort of funnel money through these British films.

But at the time, we were offered some money from one of these funds and the people running the fund were, shall we say, not whiter than white.

And then years and years later, the Inland Revenue for Her Majesty's Revenue Customs decided to investigate it and decided they didn't like what they saw. And I was prosecuted for that. I was found guilty for tax fraud and given a five-year sentence. When you get a five-year sentence in Britain, you only serve half of that in a prison. And the other half is sort of 'on-license', which is why you're out in the community or kind of supervised, but you're allowed to go and live your normal life as long as you don't break the law again.

What was it like, checking into prison?

Someone said to me, always keep a diary. One day the diary will keep you. And that was a very sensible thing to say. So, yeah, I kept notes really from day one because it was so far removed from anything I'd experienced before in my life. And it was it was this mad chaos from day one. And also entertaining, I found some of the things happening were so, so entertaining. They qualified as this kind of genius farce, really. So I just thought, well, I'm never going remember all the details. So I just wrote everything down. I wasn't thinking about a book at that point. I just wanted to write it all down. And save it for posterity. Writing it down was very therapeutic. The very act of just getting out of my head and onto the pages, was just like therapy, really. So I found it really useful. And it'd also pass the time. At the start, you're locked in for 23-hours a day. Sometimes you don't get out at all. So actually writing down everything I was thinking and feeling helped kill two or three hours a day.

And how did the experience became formative and transformative?

I had 21 months between getting out of the hellhole that it is Wandsworth and finishing my sentence in open prison. And that's when I had a lot of time to reflect and think back on my life, and not even stuff that necessarily got me into prison, but just who I was and the kind of life I led. And you think about that all the time, and then you can actually get a bit of distance from it. You can look at it in a much more analytical, objective way and see that maybe there's things in it that you were doing that just didn't make you happy. And you can think, actually, I wasn't very happy. And it's because of these things that I was doing. So maybe if I stopped doing those things, I'll be happier when I get out. You also become very conscious of time. You think about time all the time in prison. And there's a phrase which is 'the hours passed like years, and years' passed like hours'. You're very conscious that there's this whole world outside and you're not part of it.

I was very conscious that there was this or two-and-a-half years in my life, that I basically lost. And I wanted to get it back. You can't turn the clock back. But I thought to myself, and this is quite a strange way of looking at it, I thought, 'well, I'm 42 now and maybe I've got another 30 years left. Who knows.' So I thought, 'well, maybe if I stop doing all the things that are making me unhappy and I just don't do any of those things at all, then I can, over 30 years on average, get about two-and-a-half years back just by cutting out all the flim-flam and dross I don't really want to do.' So that's what I started doing.

On my wall I had a post-it note on which I wrote down every time I came up with something I thought was wasting my time or making me unhappy. I didn't want to do anymore of that? Scrawl it down on this on this post-it note. There's now a list of 10 things. This was built up over a period of maybe six months. So there were 10 things I ended up jotting down.

What's interesting is I didn't even start writing this list until I'd been in prison for about 18 months. So it took that long for me to even have the sense of perspective, to look back on the life from before, because I can see it as a very, very distinct, separate thing. It was like a little archaeological dig, in a sense. So I had to be separated from it in order to examine it effectively.

Many would try and bury the fact they spent time in prison. But Chris decided to own it.

I've been feeling fantastic and my life's been great since I got out and I've been very fortunate. A lot of people leaving prison don't have such a good time because they've struggled to get work. They struggle with relationships.

But I've done pretty well on both those fronts. I worked really hard on my book while I was away. So I had something to do when I got out, which was publishing this book. I started to write a TV series based on my experiences, and I'm also doing a podcast as well about prison life. I've had an income. I get to live with my son again. I've seen my friends. So I've had a really, really good 18 months since I got out. And I strongly think that some of that is due to the things that I've decided to cut out my life totally.

Chris has also become a vocal prison reform advocate, hosting a podcast dedicated to the subject. 'A Bit of a Stretch – The Podcast' talks to inmates, prison officers and relatives of those affected by the experience. Far from burying his stint behind bars under his manuscripts, he has used it to shape his life and career.

Conclusion

You can spend your life trying to succeed or fail in a way that looks desirable and socially acceptable to others. Or you can just be you and own your actions. Good or bad; glamorous or embarrassing and make them part of your DNA. Brands, businesses and people often find greater opportunity in setting themselves apart through their reaction to adverse circumstances than favourable ones. So make every twist and turn part of your strength and secret sauce.

CHAPTER SIXTEEN

Suffering alone isn't as productive as suffering together

'It's like having to admit that you're definitely, totally, inexcusably incompetent' – the secret voice inside all of our heads.

On community. We're familiar with the saying 'a problem shared is a problem halved'. But this chapter goes beyond sharing and explores what happens when you build whole communities around your problem.

> **Myth** – If I accept help, I'm not capable enough.
> **Truth** – There is value in community and asking for help.

Why is it that asking for help is often a less preferential option to getting a colonoscopy? Whether you're driving around lost in an unknown neighbourhood or confronted with a project at work that feels like a complicated German grammar lesson, turning to YouTube or Google can only put off the inevitable question for so long. Eventually, all of us will hit a dead end and need to mutter that four-letter word that sounds like a painful admission of guilt and shame, to our own ears at least: Help.

Myth

Most of us who are of working age will have grown up with a certain shame attached to admitting you can't do something, that you don't know something or that you are not able to complete a task alone. Whether it's a domestic task, a life decision or something at work. Our initial instinct is to nod along, give the impression that we are in control and then quietly panic and blag our way through.

Here are some assumptions we make to avoid asking for help. Some of these might even sound familiar to you.

- **Assumption 1:** It's a sign of weakness. If I can't do it on my own, I'm not smart enough.
- **Assumption 2:** Allowing someone else to help me means I lose control of the situation.

- **Assumption 3:** If I receive support from them then I will have to reciprocate further down the line. What if I can't return the favour? What if I don't want to return the favour?
- **Assumption 4:** If I ask for the support of others, I am burdening them. They are just as busy as me so how could they find the time to help out?
- **Assumption 5:** I am the only one that can do it my way. It's easier and quicker for me to do it, than to train or teach someone else to help me.

Do any of these ring a bell? There are many other assumptions, real or made up, that prevent us from 'reaching out'. As adults, we are not hard-wired to ask for help or, for that matter, to receive it in a way which feels empowering to us.

This seems to be something which we unlearn as we grow up. Because we fall over ourselves with offers of help to children. Often met with an offended refusal. 'Do you need help putting on your coat, wiping your bum, cutting up those pizza slices, doing your homework, pouring that milk?' 'No!' Other times, it's the only word you will hear on repeat from a frustrated toddler trying to get to grips with the world.

Once you hit a certain age though, adults stop asking. They start assuming you know what they know. Then you start getting paid to know stuff. To do stuff. And promoted if you seem to know more than those around you. Knowledge is power. And the admission of the lack of that knowledge risks making yourself look less powerful.

It doesn't help that we've suffered some pretty bad role models on that front.

From Margaret Thatcher to Alex Ferguson, from Simon Cowell to Dominic Cummings. Their power is derived from the impression that they are infallible. Not knowing something, openly asking for help, admitting to a weakness is not an option for them. And by proxy, this has become a flawed benchmark for the rest of society. It's worth noting that many dated leadership traits are derived from equally dated, male stereotypes. Stiff upper lip… to succeed, to be admired, to progress… you must go it alone. Men were trapped by it, women forced to adopt to it.

Truth

Luckily that myth has started to make its way into the history books. It might have been a truth in the past. But the times are changing and, depending on what country you live in, vulnerability, humanity, admission of flaws and weaknesses and actively asking for help are signs of progressive leadership.

It's hard to imagine Barack Obama doing anything other than applaud a member of his team for admitting a blind spot on a foreign policy issue, or a knowledge gap on human trafficking in the Baltic states. In fact, here is what he had to say about asking for help.

'Don't be afraid to ask questions. Don't be afraid to ask for help when you need it. I do it every day. Asking for help isn't a sign of weakness, it's a sign of strength. It shows you have the courage to admit when you don't know something, and learn something new.' (Obama, 2009).

Collaboration, community, and compassion sit at the heart of the ask for or the offer of help. And these are, thankfully, becoming the trademarks of progressive leadership.

Human beings are wired to want to give help. It's one of the richest sources of self-esteem, and it has the potential to be a real win-win. Helping is rewarding for people because they like to be supportive and connect with other people.

A Stanford University study highlighted this in an experiment conducted in order to understand the difference between asking for help vs giving help (Flynn and Lake, 2008). This study was conducted by Frank Flynn, associate professor of organizational behaviour at Stanford Graduate School of Business. Here are his conclusions.

In the first two studies, participants were issued instructions to ask favours of people on campus after estimating how many people they thought would agree to help with their requests. 'Participants asked to borrow strangers' cell phones in order to make calls back to the experimenter, solicited individuals to fill out questionnaires, and asked students to help them find the campus gym – a favour that required obliging students to walk with a participant for at least two blocks in the direction of the gym.'

The researchers found that participants consistently overestimated by 50 per cent the number of people they'd have to ask to get a certain number to agree with each request. 'Participants were initially horrified at the prospect of going out and asking people for such things,' says

Lake. 'But they'd bound back in to the lab afterward with big smiles, saying, "I can't believe how nice people were!".

Two follow up studies confirmed these behaviours and reactions. When given specific scenarios, participants responded differently depending on whether they were in the role of a potential helper or the one who needed the help. If you were asking for help, you thought you were more likely to be turned down than those with help on offer. Even more importantly, askers said they thought it would be much easier for others to refuse their request than did potential helpers.

'That's really the mechanism explaining the effect,' says Flynn. 'People's underestimation of others' willingness to comply is driven by their failure to diagnose these feelings of social obligation on the part of others.' (Rigoglioso, 2008).

THE TOOL

From (knowledge) gap to (learning) curve

Gaps suggest you should know something but don't. Curves suggest an active learning experience. Asking for help should always be about the latter, because learning always occurs on the fringes of knowledge.

So what do you do if you need to approach a colleague, a neighbour, a friend or your boss for help?

Commonly used, confidence-destroying and less impactful tactics of asking for help include treating it like a knowledge gap, as illustrated in table 16.1:

TABLE 16.1   Treating lack of knowledge as a gap and a problem

GAP
Let your challenge linger
Apologize for not knowing
Focus on what you're not able to do
Not showing your attempts at solving the problem
Implying you can't do it and maybe someone else should
Keep the help received to yourself

This becomes a destructive way of not just tackling a challenge, but also managing the relationships around you. Because you feel on your back foot, or even at fault for not knowing, you aren't giving yourself full credit for the efforts you have made, what you do know, and the ground you have covered, even if it didn't lead to a solution. Instead, approach the situation with a sense of entitlement to learn more and to demand support. And don't forget, if you're struggling it's likely someone else is too. Never overestimate what other people know! It's about scaling that curve in a positive and inclusive manner, as Table 16.2 shows.

TABLE 16.2   Turning lack of knowledge into an opportunity and upward trajectory

GAP	CURVE
Let your challenge linger	Be fast to ask
Apologize for not knowing	Never apologize. It's a curve, not a gap!
Focus on what you're not able to do	Explain what you know so far
Not showing your attempts at solving the problem	Show what you've tried so far, even if you know it's wrong
Implying you can't do it and maybe someone else should	Ask to be shown how to do it yourself, or to stay involved
Keep the help received to yourself	Share what you've learnt with others

The difference between treating a challenge like a learning curve, instead of a gap, is that you are actively managing and sourcing the input of others while taking the learnings as a positive step forward. You still retain ownership, you are still driving the proverbial bus, but you allow yourself to grow instead of feeling diminished. Involving others in your journey not only gives you a greater shot at successfully completing your challenge, but also the opportunity to share what you have learnt with others who might be facing similar obstacles.

THE INSPIRATION

Lucy Rocca, Founder of Soberistas

Lucy Rocca was an outwardly successful person. She was a mother of one, had recently completed a law degree and was the life and soul of the party when she went out. Drinking alcohol was a big part of her life. She admits that she couldn't really have a good time socializing unless she was drinking. And she regularly drank more than her friends. Following the separation from her daughter's father, her drinking became more prominent at home as well. A day wouldn't go by when she wasn't holding a glass of wine in her hand.

But she was functioning. Excelling at work. Juggling her responsibilities at home. Regularly running half marathons. Nothing was going off the boiler. Until one night, as her daughter was staying with her father, she went out, started drinking and woke up in A&E not remembering a thing that had happened. This was her trigger moment to rebuild. She knew she couldn't afford another incident like this. The idea of embarrassing herself was bad enough, but the thought of doing this in front of her daughter's schoolmates and their parents was unbearable. So Lucy stopped drinking overnight. She didn't join AA because she didn't identify as being a 'park bench alcoholic'. Doctors had previously seemed unperturbed when she mentioned the regularity with which she drank. Lucy knuckled down all alone, feeling too ashamed to talk to anybody about her situation. She started writing a blog about her journey. Which started to attract quite a lot of attention. Because other women were feeling the same way Lucy was. Not able to ask for help, as they didn't see themselves as hardcore alcoholics, even though their relationship with alcohol was clearly a troubled one.

When I set up my WordPress blog, it attracted quite a lot of followers. And so I was communicating with people who had gone through similar things. And it was that, that was just so mind-blowing; to realize that it wasn't just me and it wasn't my fault. You know, it was just a huge relief to know that there were other people who'd been through it. And who understood how that felt. Because I'd never met people like that before.

Lucy was clearly on to something, so she founded an online community for women who didn't like their relationship with alcohol. She called it Soberistas. A place for women to support each other, help each other, succeed together. Forgoing the usual connotations of an alcohol support group, women were able to be themselves, unashamed, unjudged, and motivated by each other towards better and healthier lifestyle choices. Lucy's and Soberistas' approach is a great example of how to tackle the unknown through the support of a community, where the curve is very much scaled together and learnings are shared in a positive and supportive environment.

I realized at the start of my recovery journey that if I was going to spend the rest of my life bumping into drink, and thinking I was missing out on something, it was going to be pretty miserable and I might as well carry on drinking. So I came to the conclusion that I needed to make it positive and that I had to be happy about not drinking. Otherwise, my life is just going to be marred by this constant feeling of deprivation and missing out. At Alcoholics Anonymous you're carrying around this horrible, shameful label for the rest of your life, which makes you feel [terrible]. Basically, I wanted Soberistas to be a positive place to stop drinking. And it is a positive thing to stop drinking. Focus on the gains, not the losses.

But I actually realized from Soberistas that the way people support and nurture each other is selfless and amazing. And it has restored my faith in people massively. You know, watching how much people give, even people who have been sober for five years still on the website because they want to help others. And the idea that when there are lots and lots of people all going through the same experience, it makes it a nice experience, rather than it being lonely and scary. It's really important to feel part of a tribe. It is a fundamental human need to feel as if we belong. And that's what I've learnt.

Conclusion

The act of asking for help and considering it a positive step forwards will no doubt sit uncomfortably with most of us. Because we perceive it to highlight shortcomings or gaps in our knowledge and experience, we suffer alone and launch ourselves into downward spirals of negative thoughts and behaviours. By challenging this mindset and accepting that everyone is entitled to support, for themselves and the team or community they are apart of, and that this support in fact makes us stronger and more capable, we open ourselves up to a whole new possibility of recovery, progress and positive momentum towards a sustainable future.

PART THREE

Comebacks are for life

CHAPTER SEVENTEEN

Rebuilds are a process, not a project

'Most things in life don't go exactly to plan, you've just got to roll with it' – the conclusion many of us will come to if we've overcome a setback.

On recovering from a setback. It's rarely a fait accompli. It's a process that can take months, years, sometimes a lifetime. This chapter explores the best ways of ensuring your comeback stays on track.

Myth – There is a beginning and an end to every rebuild.
Truth – Rebuilds simply transition through different phases.

Myth

We like to think of challenges as little or big parcels of trouble that are experienced, processed, solved, packed up neatly with a bow tied around them and filed into our mental storage compartment, hopefully never to be revisited.

Setbacks are mostly unwelcome happenings that are bid farewell at the soonest possible opportunity. This very common reaction to a challenge is in no small part caused by the following misconceptions we have come to believe about what setbacks are and who can handle them best:

1 Setbacks are linear and have a beginning and an endpoint.
2 But some setbacks you can never recover from.
3 You are either a resilient person or not.
4 Those people who are resilient experience less stress and worry in life.

These opinions haven't been helpful in demystifying resilience and creating a culture that treats it for what it is: a skill to be learnt and mastered through practise.

The reason we feel so passionately about the process of rebuilding is because it's one of the most democratic experiences out there. Yet still so untapped and misunderstood. Everyone, without exception, will experience something that goes wrong in life or in business. Some things big, some things small, some you may not even be aware of at first. The situations will vary greatly. But they all create unforeseen change, instability, trauma or stress. And resilience is our ability to bounce back and rebuild from these curveballs in a constructive way over sustained periods of time; and even grow from them. It's a deliberate action and thinking pattern of taking these events and turning them in fuel, not despair.

As the UK Government Office for Science aptly put it: 'Resilience is considered a mediator or moderator between adversity and well-being' (Bennett, 2015).

That skill though is still reserved for the few, because until now, unless you got lucky in the genetic lottery and just popped into this world as a resilient mensch, you're unlikely to be taught how to bounce back in the same way you might be taught presentation skills, coding skills, or even reading and writing skills. That is to say, systematically explained, practised and perfected.

Angela Duckworth is an American psychologist who studies what makes people successful in life. In her bestseller *Grit: The Power of Passion and Perseverance* Duckworth argued that the prime indicator of achievement isn't IQ or talent, but the possession of 'grit', the ability to dig in and keep going despite the headwinds. It's treating challenges like a marathon (because they come thick and fast throughout life), not a sprint. She also points out that despite the impact 'grit' skills have on children's academic and social trajectory, we still know relatively little about them as it's not a topic the academic world has yet embraced or applied to lived schoolroom experiences.

Whether you're sitting in second grade, in the board room or at home, nobody should live in fear of change or challenge. Everybody should understand how setbacks can be tackled, little by little, to a positive resolve. It's teachable. And, more importantly, resilience can have a culminative effect. The more you flex your rebuilding muscles, the better you will become at managing the process. It won't make you immune from worry or stress, but you will see it in a different light and use those experiences to greater effect.

Truth

As the Roman philosopher Lucius Seneca is reported to have once observed, 'difficulties strengthen the mind, as labour does the body'.

Everyone has the ability to turn a setback into a comeback. Resilience breeds resilience breeds resilience. It's a cumulative effect. Like a muscle, it becomes stronger the more you exercise it. This isn't to suggest that you become more immune or less involved in setbacks, but you become better at spotting them and working with them, not against them. That is why the idea of simply being a resilient person or not being a resilient person is flawed. It's only when you're faced with obstacles, stress, and other environmental threats that resilience emerges and you learn to respond to it.

Setbacks come and go in different guises. Some are acute in their nature, requiring an intensive burst of work (a divorce, redundancy, an accident), others are more systemic and they stay with us for a longer time (rebuilding a community, working through depression, rebuilding a company's culture). Some setbacks resolve themselves, just to reappear some time later (like cancer or addiction). The point is, something is always lurking. It's not a negative view of the world, but simply a recognition of how prevalent and common setbacks are and therefore how important it is to learn how to manage them.

Following the death of her ex-husband who had succumbed to the by-effects of intravenous drug use, Eilene Zimmerman wrote in *The New York Times*:

> It turns out that awful time in my life was good training for a pandemic, for political and social upheaval, for economic and financial uncertainty. The experience taught me that I never really know what's going to happen next. I plan as best I can, but now I'm far more able to pivot my thinking. I have the capacity to cope with more of life's unexpected slings and arrows, to accept the difficulties I face and keep going, even though it can be hard (Zimmerman, 2020).

With every setback carrying its own particular hallmarks and therefore requiring a different infrastructure to solve, it's easy to get lost in the particularities of each case. What we have set out to achieve with *The Rebuilders* is to find commonalities that are useful for everyone to consider, no matter the situation. With that in mind, we want to conclude with a few overall observations and thoughts.

Firstly, it's important to take a holistic view. If you can imagine a little proverbial cursor moving across the situation that is causing you anxiety, worry and fear, take it to the toolbar at the top of your window, select 'view' and press 'zoom out'. Click eight times. This will show you what else is happening around you, in other parts of your life, in other parts of your mind, as well as across time. Contextualizing your situation will help you see the bigger picture and this will help you realize that what you are experiencing right now is not the only thing that defines you, your career, your relationships and your future. It is merely a component. The wider context will also help you make decisions, set priorities and boundaries and interpret the information you have in the most constructive way.

There is a second point on the holistic view of rebuilds. It's easy to get stuck on the challenge alone. For example, trying to save a failing business. With all the good will in the world, it's impossible to achieve such turnarounds by staring at spreadsheets all day, sitting in endless meetings and conversations. You're not just in a relationship with your challenge, but also with yourself. Consider what you are doing to support your physical health, your emotional health, your relationships and any support you might want to seek out to help with any of those areas in your life. Resilience requires you to tap into all of these aspects, so take good care of yourself, it will make the rest a little easier.

In 2015, Peter Limbach and Florian Sonnenburg conducted a piece of research for the Cologne Centre of Financial Research entitled 'Does CEO Fitness Matter?' Their findings demonstrated that a CEO's physical fitness is associated with higher firm profitability and higher M&A announcement returns, in line with other known benefits of physical fitness such as stress management, cognitive functioning, and overall job performance. The study measured firm performance in companies whose CEOs had run a marathon within the past 12 months. They also showed that physically fit CEOs 'are associated with significantly higher return on assets and more free cash flow'. Additionally, 'abnormal stock returns to M&A announcements are significantly higher, and are less likely to be negative, when the bidding firm's boss is fit' (Limbach and Sonnenburg, 2015).

THE TOOL – FLEXING YOUR RESILIENCE MUSCLES EVERYDAY WITH THE THREE GS

Training yourself to think a certain way is no different to working out to strengthen your core, or taking vitamins to keep healthy, or writing down a to-do list to keep you on track.

To ensure you are keeping yourself on track whichever peak or trough you're in, whether you're in the middle of a crisis or not, here are three simple things you can build into your daily thought process. It needn't take long, you needn't dig deep, but these prompts might just help keep you focused on the right experiences.

Goal for today

Setting yourself an achievable goal for the day will create an immediate sense of accomplishment and positive momentum. Our goals are often set so far in the future that they can take weeks, months, even years to achieve. Setting yourself a target and feeling a small sense of accomplishment each day will help trigger new behaviours, guide your focus and help you sustain that momentum in everyday life.

Gratitude from today

A lot of things can go wrong during 24 hours. We've been there many times! And it's easy to feel the frustration of everything that could have been (a lot) better weighing heavy on your shoulders. Sometimes it takes a deliberate effort to identify the one thing that was actually pretty good. Whether it was a corridor conversation that put a smile on your face, a tiny win in a massive battle, a good cup of coffee, a nice walk or run, or something your kids or pet did that made you feel happy. If you look hard enough there is something good in every day. Reminding yourself of this at the end of the day will ensure your negative emotions have a positive counterbalance, which is so important as you work your way through a rebuild. Reminding yourself of the good in your life will definitely give you that extra push to power through the tough times.

Good health everyday

This feels so obvious you could almost write it off as trivial. But it's so important to remember to look after your health. And it's often the first thing we sacrifice when the going gets tough. Bad food, too much of the wrong stimulant, no exercise, no time to clear your head. All of these things won't bring you down in isolation, but compounded with the other stuff you're dealing with, will have an impact on how resilient you feel. Physically and mentally. The analogy of 'put your oxygen mask on before you help the person next to you' rings true here. The person next to you is your rebuild.

Resilience comes in many different shapes and sizes. Because every setback is unique. But it's something each of us can master, it's a mindset and a process everyone can learn and use. Some days will demand a more intensive engagement with these skills (when you're in crisis mode), other days it's just being conscious of how we view ourselves and the world around us and keep our resilience muscles active and ready to go.

THE INSPIRATION

We have had the privilege of speaking to many inspiring individuals while researching this book and producing our podcast. At this point we didn't want to single out any particular story, but instead reflect on a few things we have learnt on our journey.

As this chapter suggests, we have discovered that rebuilds are rarely a done and dusted affair. And that isn't a bad thing. Bringing something back to life that was broken, fragile and in need of total reengineering is something that changes you. It will challenge your assumptions, the truths that have gone unquestioned for much of your life. It will take you to the brink and you will have to make choices, sacrifices and leaps of faith that you may not have thought yourself capable of at the outset of your journey. Through this process, you become more compassionate with yourself, with others, with the world around you and you start to rebuild not just the thing that was broken, but the world and the context you exist in. You will value different character traits, prioritize different needs, maybe become a little more direct and honest and comfortable in disagreeing with people you were obsessed with pleasing. You will start to make different choices in all aspects of your life. Your work, your relationships, your health, your friends, your career. How you do something becomes as meaningful and what you do.

Rebuilds require maintenance. Best practice, enthusiastic discipline and conviction will support whatever form your rebuild takes next. Don't try and forget the challenges you fought hard to overcome. Once the initial problem, trauma or situation has settled, it's always tempting to forget it ever happened. This isn't to suggest you should dwell on the past. Instead, keep the habits that exercised your resilience muscles. Even when times are good. They will make the good times better as well as the tough ones more manageable.

Lastly, share your story. It helps you process your journey, it reminds you how far you have come and it will serve as inspiration and comfort to others facing a tough time. Problems don't have to be identical in order to share a solution or a helpful approach. That is why we wrote this book. Because, at the end of the day, rebuilding is something we can learn from each other.

Conclusion

Resilience is a skill anyone can choose and learn. And like most things in life, the more you exercise and practise these skills and habits, the more confident you become in managing adversity and setbacks. Focus on the day ahead, the things you can control and look after yourself and your team. Progress is rarely linear so don't be disheartened by twists and turns.

Rebuilding
is the future

On setting future generations up for success. Each of us will experience our fair share of setbacks during a lifetime. Knowing how to approach these with confidence and resilience will dictate how likely we are to turn them into comebacks. This chapter discusses the importance of teaching our children the values of rebuilding and some tools to get started young.

Myth – Rebuilding is a skill you only need if something goes wrong.

Truth – It's a life skill for everyone! The earlier you learn it, the better equipped you are.

Myth

'If you are not prepared to be wrong, you will never come up with anything original,' said Sir Ken Robinson, professor and educator who devoted decades to improving the formal education system (Robinson, 2006). The skills of rebuilding and resilience are integral to living a happy and healthy life which is reason enough to embed them in the next generation. But there is a more fundamental reason for equipping them to face life's setbacks. Working through failure is vital for innovation and progress to occur. For us and for every generation to come, the ability to innovate and to think originally and creatively will be an integral part of our futures and theirs.

Kids are our future, sang Whitney Houston. As well as being a masterful pop song, Whitney was spot on about the role of the next generation in shaping our lives. Whether we have kids, know kids or simply walk past them occasionally on the street, our lives will be influenced by them in decades to come. While humanity hasn't gone to hell in a handcart quite yet, there are quite a few urgent items to fix on our collective to-do list. With climate change, global pandemics and the unknown impacts of web 3.0 and AI on society, there is a large amount for the next generation to tackle. As Whitney says, to ensure the kids are equipped to tackle what lays ahead we need to teach them well and let them lead the way.

As far back as 2006, Sir Ken stated his belief that creativity was as important as literacy and should be taken as seriously (Robinson, 2006). Since then, the need for innovation, diverse thinking, and creative problem solving has only intensified. The future of work is changing thick and fast and an estimated 85 per cent of the jobs in 2030 haven't been invented yet (Dell Technologies, 2018). This means children currently in school are preparing for unknown jobs, in industries that don't exist, tackling problems that haven't been identified yet. McKinsey believes that almost no-one will be unaffected: 'Artificial intelligence and auto-mation will make this shift as significant as the mechaniza-tion in prior generations of agriculture and manufacturing. While some jobs will be lost, and many others created, almost all will change.' (McKinsey & Company, 2022). In 2021 McKinsey surveyed 18,000 people across 15 coun-tries to define the skills citizens will need in the future of work and it reads like a description of the rebuilders covered in this book. They include grit, persistence, coping with uncertainty, structured problem solving, mental flexi-bility, courage and risk-taking, adaptability, ability to learn, adopting a different perspective and resolving conflicts, to name but a few (Dondi et al, 2021).

Speaking to employers reveals the same picture. Craig Fenton, Senior Google Executive, has been the Head of Strategy and Operations for UK and Ireland for five years, as well as a long-time investor in disruptive technologies. With a view from within one of the world's most successful tech businesses he has a strong sense of what skills are needed moving forwards.

The skill I think that separates the good from the great in this day and age is creativity – which underpins a comfort with change and ambiguity. To embrace a life, in which we will never be truly masters of anything, because it just changes too quickly. To find excitement in that sort of continuous cycle of learning. To see around the corners. To imagine a future that's different than today, and then go create it. These are all different ways of describing creativity. In business, we just call it by a different name. We call it innovation (Source 6).

Like Sir Ken, Craig highlights the role that dealing with set backs and failure has in enabling innovation. He points to Google's Project Aristotle, a study conducted in 2012 which aimed to decode the difference between good teams, great teams and exceptionally high-performing teams at Google (Source 7). The study found that peak performance boiled down to one key factor called psychological safety.

> Psychological safety is a context in which bravery exists. The willingness to take risks and fail, and know that your colleagues next to you will pick you up, pat you on the back for trying, and move forward with you, that you're not punished in that sense, that well-calculated risks are rewarded even and perhaps especially if they fail, because you learn more from the failures than you do if you succeed. If you try something that succeeds, you already knew the answer to begin with. Obviously, you've just confirmed it. But failure moves you forward in some way (Source 8).

But we can relax because kids are learning all this in school right? Not exactly. While teachers and schools do a super-human job of supporting, caring for and teaching our children, the core education system in most countries is not designed to promote the mindset and attitudes that support resilience and rebuilding.

In Craig's view as both a dad and a tech guy, intelligence is far broader than what we educate and test for. 'Creativity is becoming as or more important than classical intelligence. Knowledge is a commodity and much of it is perishable, quickly becoming obsolete' (Source 9). The main challenge is that the primary measure of academic progress in schools is still examinations and assessments that reward knowledge recall and exam technique, and punish failure. Neither what is being measured nor how it is being measured encourages trial and error, innovation or learning by experimentation. Craig has interviewed hundreds of young people for roles at Google and believes that great examination results or degrees from the top universities don't always correlate with the skills needed in a fast-moving modern workplace. Time and again he finds that classical education pathways miss a whole breadth of talent who are equally if not more capable in the workplace.

A view from inside the UK educational establishment confirms this view. Sammy Wright is an english teacher, founder of the sixth form at Southmoor Academy, Sunderland and former member of the Social Mobility Commission with a particular focus on improving educational outcomes for children from low socio-economic backgrounds. The current approach to exams and assessment that 'rewards recall and time at home to revise and drill' has several drawbacks in his view. In our conversations, he explained that the system restricts diversity and social mobility because the testing approach lends itself to a very narrow range of attributes that tend to align with those who are 'white, middle class, like books and have parents who are professionals, who went to university themselves'. He continues:

> This has left me with a really lasting sense that what people call success in education isn't always success. It's luck a lot of the time, it's ease, it's whether or not you happen to be the person that the education system is looking for. Over the years, I've seen a lot of young people who are not that person but who have many qualities that I personally lack, and yet they don't have a sense of ease as they move their way through education.

The second of his criticisms is that exams don't allow for deep or considered thought and instead reward the ability to sound plausible on the spot.

> It doesn't reward people who test out their ideas to make sure that they're not wrong. It rewards the ability to come up with something that looks plausible rather than properly testing and investigating what you're doing and acknowledging when you may not be right. To me, that's almost the opposite of intelligence, because to be right all the time is someone who is maybe overconfident, and maybe hasn't properly assessed the pros and cons of what they're doing.

Whether it be in politics or in the workplace, we have all come across the type of character that Mr Wright describes. Sammy raises the question of what we want in the leaders of tomorrow: 'Do we want the people with the glib, quick answers or do we want the deep thinkers? I think we certainly know which we have, and we might recognize that hasn't necessarily always gone that well.'

Truth

Most of us aren't in a position to be altering the education system but there are still things we can do to foster the type of resilience and creativity that formal education may not. After all, kids have all the raw materials they need, we just need to know how to preserve them. As Sir Ken so vehemently believed 'All kids have tremendous talents and we squander them ruthlessly' (Robinson, 2006).

One of the most important factors in giving children the resilience they need to deal with set backs is a strong sense of their own self-worth. The belief that they are good, valid and valued people regardless of the outcome of what they are doing. If something goes wrong, it is just a thing that went wrong. If they fail at something, it is just a failure. These things shouldn't dent their integral sense of their own value. Missteps and mistakes don't make them bad people. Dr Maryhan Baker is a psychologist and parenting expert, as well as a mother of two, who specializes in supporting children, teens, and young adults struggling with low confidence and anxiety. She also has a podcast called 'How not to screw up your kids' which is absolutely gold for anyone attempting to muddle through parenting. In her interview with us, she spoke about children's confidence:

> They need to believe at their core, they're a nice, decent person, a fun person to be around. When they have that belief then when they're faced with situations that feel slightly outside their comfort zone, they don't get caught up in the judgement around 'what might people think if I can't do this? People will not think that I'm particularly

good.' Instead, they approach things from a position of, 'I know that I'm a decent person, and if I fail or if I succeed, that's not a reflection on who I am, but on this particular situation.' It's like the foundations of a house. You can't build in academia and all the other layers, if you haven't got that solid foundation that you believe you are fundamentally a good person.

Another important factor is for children to believe that their skill, talents and abilities can be built on, that they aren't fixed or something immutable that they were born with. If they don't yet know or aren't yet good at something, they need to believe they potential to get better. As we know from Chapter 9, this is called a 'growth mindset'. When children have a growth mindset they relish challenges as a chance to learn and develop and when they experience failures or make errors they process them as positive learning opportunities. With a 'fixed mindset', children believe their abilities are fixed and are more likely to experience setbacks negatively as a judgement on their talents. Those with a 'growth mindset' progress faster because they worry less about looking smart and put more energy into learning (Dweck, 2006).

So whether you are raising kids or just hanging out with them occasionally, we have pulled together some ways to support children in developing these vital skills.

Praise the process not the outcome

This is one of the core principles of growth mindset, now commonly adopted in many schools. It involves rewarding and praising children for the energy and effort they put in, not only for getting scores they get out. Praising effort encourages children to continue to work hard, strive to learn and is proven to improve future performance. This could involve praising them for studying hard for the test or for answering all the test questions. Research conducted by Dweck amongst twelve-year-olds showed that children praised for their intelligence went on to perform worse in future tests. In contrast, children praised for their effort went on to perform better (Mueller and Dweck, 1998). This isn't about dropping standards and pretending that everyone has done wonderfully. It is about encouraging children to continue to be resourceful in their learning and to believe they can keep getting better.

Destigmatize failure

Role modelling that failures are commonplace and not terminal, goes a long way to helping children accept them as a natural part of life. It encourages them to experiment and not get too disheartened when things don't go as planned. Head teacher Heather Hanbury at Wimbledon High School went as far as creating 'failure week' to build resilience and encourage girls to embrace risk. The pupils were encouraged to try new activities and explore how it felt to fail, as well as hearing talks from parents around their own missteps.

> The girls need to learn how to fail well – and how to get over it and cope with it. Fear of failing can be really crippling and stop the girls doing things they really want to do. The pupils are hugely successful but can sometimes overreact to failure even though it can sometimes be enormously beneficial to them (Source 16).

As with many of these tips and tools, adults can benefit too. When Craig Fenton at Google noticed that his team meeting was becoming a showboating session where people only presented their best work, he instituted a section where they shared their 'glorious failures' of the week. His aim was to 'destigmatize and convert failure from a negative to a positive thereby encouraging greater creativity and innovation' (Source 17).

The aim in these examples isn't to eradicate failure and pretend that everything is always hunky dory, but rather to create environments where failure is understood to be a vital part of the learning experience and not to be avoided.

Mind your language

Language plays a big part in how we interpret and frame events in our mind, particularly while children are still developing and learning. Careful use of language can help children view challenges and set-backs in a motivating rather than a demotivating light. Dr Dweck talks about the power of using 'not yet' rather than 'failed' in exams and assessments to denote to children that they can still pass in future if they continue to work hard. 'If you get a failing grade, you think, I'm nothing, I'm nowhere. But if you get the grade "not yet" you understand that you're on a learning curve. It gives you a path into the future' (Dweck, 2014). Being similarly mindful about how we praise success has a powerful effect. In our conversations, Dr Maryhan advises 'saying what you see' when remarking on children's efforts. Not going over the top and bestowing lashing of praise all the time but dropping the superlatives and praising what the child is actually doing. Rather than 'Oh, my God, that's incredible. You are phenomenal.' instead, actually praise what you see. 'I'm really impressed that you sat up at the table when I asked you, because that showed great listening.' By being really specific rather than lavishly over praising, Dr Maryhan says we are likely to get more of the behaviours we would like to see more often.

Don't swoop in to solve

For anyone who has watched a child grapple with a tough time at school or watched a toddler try to put their shoe on the wrong foot for 10 solid minutes, this is the toughest tip to hear. To build their confidence and resilience children need the space to solve things for themselves. If we constantly swoop in to rescue, solve and smooth life's wrinkles they will never develop the resourcefulness and self-belief that they've 'got this'. This can run counter to a parent's strong urge to protect children and smooth their way in life, but as Dr Maryhan says 'confidence is an inside job. It doesn't matter how much we praise our children, we can't give our children confidence, it has to come from within. It comes from stepping back, allowing our children to take calculated risks and giving them the opportunity to learn.'

Allow them to make choices

One way of not swooping in to solve problems is to encourage children to make choices for themselves. Dr Maryhan suggests actively encouraging even small children to make choices and decisions where they can. Do they want broccoli or peas for their dinner? Do they want to wear the red top or the blue one? Even the age-old disagreement over whether or not they wear their coats outside. Encouraging them to make choices builds their sense of responsibility and helps them to understand the consequences of their actions. The consequence of not wearing the raincoat may be that they get a little wet but they start to build a sense that decisions have different outcomes. For older children where we want to step in Dr Maryan suggests supporting them to problem-solve by themselves. If they have had an argument with a friend, ask them what they think might be a good course of action rather than dictate what they should do. All these practice runs at solving life's dilemmas will establish confidence in their own choices as life gets trickier and the set backs more high stake.

Conclusion

With children, as with all of us, all set backs teach something. Life may have slings and arrows ready to hurl at us from a young age but every bump in the road helps us to navigate the next bump we come across. In the wonderful words of Dr Maryhan:

> When children worry 'but what if I fail? What if I can't do it? I'm just going to be back to where I was.' I'll go to great lengths to say, 'You can never go back to where you were because you're a different person. You've learned, you've progressed. While it might feel like it's a setback, you're still moving forward, because you've had the courage to try.' And that makes you fundamentally changed.

Sound advice for every rebuilder.

References

Chapter 1

Berman, R (2022) Business apocalypse: Fifty-two Percent of Fortune 500 Companies from the Year 2000 Are Extinct, Courageous, available from: https://ryanberman.com/glossary/business-apocalypse/ (archived at https://perma.cc/BA77-VBVJ) [Last accessed: 13 January 2022]

Cady, S, Jacobs, J, Koller, R, and Spalding, J (2014) The change formula: Myth, legend, or lore, *OD Practitioner*, [46] (3), pp 32–39

Economy, P (2019) 17 Powerfully Inspiring Quotes From Ruth Bader Ginsburg, Inc., 12 January, available from: https://www.inc.com/peter-economy/17-powerfully-inspiring-quotes-from-ruth-bader-ginsburg.html (archived at https://perma.cc/RFA6-7P9N) [Last accessed: 13 January 2022]

Gibbs, S (2014) Google Glass advice: how to avoid being a glasshole, The Guardian, 19 February, available from: https://www.theguardian.com/technology/2014/feb/19/google-glass-advice-smartglasses-glasshole (archived at https://perma.cc/N6Q5-WNLX) [Last accessed: 13 January 2022]

Keynes, J (1924) *A Tract on Monetary Reform,* Macmillan and Co, London

Chapter 2

Csikszentmihalyi, M (1990) Flow: The psychology of optimal experience, Harper and Row, New York

Draper, T (1900) The Bemis History and Genealogy: Being an Account, in Greater Part, of the Descendants of Joseph Bemis of Watertown, Massachusetts, The Stanley Taylor Co., San Francisco

Garis, M (2020) How to *Actually* Take Things Day by Day, According to a Psychologist, Well + Good, 23 April, available from: https://www.wellandgood.com/how-to-take-thing-day-by-day/ (archived at https://perma.cc/EDC9-QB8E) [Last accessed: 17 December 2021]

Killingsworth, M and Gilbert, D (2010) A Wandering Mind is an Unhapp y Mind, Science Magazine, [330] November 2010, pp 932

MarketData (2017) The U.S. Meditation Market [Online], available from: https://www.marketresearch.com/Marketdata-Enterprises-Inc-v416/Meditation-11905615/?progid=91593 (archived at https://perma.cc/M2FA-L42U) [Last accessed: 10 January 2022]

Rapaport, D (2021) Exclusive: Tiger Woods discusses golf future in first in-depth interview since car accident, Golf Digest, 29 November, available from: https://www.golfdigest.com/story/tiger-woods-exclusive-interview (archived at https://perma.cc/6GND-BS64) [Last accessed: 10 January 2022]

Walton, A (2015) 7 Ways Meditation Can Actually Change the Brain, Forbes, 9 February, available from: https://www.forbes.com/sites/alicegwalton/2015/02/09/7-ways-meditation-can-actually-change-the-brain/?sh=2834e8c41465 (archived at https://perma.cc/LUY8-K949) [Last accessed: 23 December 2021]

Chapter 3

Artino, A (2012) Academic self-efficacy: from educational theory to instructional practice, Perspectives on Medical Education, [1], pp 76–85

Kashdan, T (2009) Curious?: Discover the Missing Ingredient to a Fulfilling Life, William Morrow & Co, New York

Lieberman, M, Inagaki, T, Tabibnia, G, and Crockett, M (2011) Subjective Responses to Emotional Stimuli During Labeling, Reapp raisal, and Distraction, Emotion, [11], pp 468–480

McGowan, S, and Behar, E (2013) A Preliminary Investigation of Stimulus Control Training for Worry: Effects on Anxiety and Insomnia, *Behavior Modification*, [37] (1), pp 90–112

Purbasari Horton, A (2019) 5 mindfulness techniques for letting go of control, Fast Company, 11 November, available from: https://www.fastcompany.com/90424137/5-mindfulness-techniques-for-letting-go-of-control (archived at https://perma.cc/BDR9-QJR9) [Last accessed: 10 January 2022]

Raghunathan, R (2016a) If You're So Smart, Why Aren't You Happy?, Portfolio, New York

Raghunathan, R (2016b) Why Losing Control Can Make You Happier, Greater Good Magazine, 28 September, available from: https://greatergood.berkeley.edu/article/item/why_losing_control_make_you_happier (archived at https://perma.cc/4B8W-GLRZ) [Last accessed: 10 January 2022]

Wygal, W (1940) We Plan Our Own Worship Services: Business girls practice the act and the art of group worship, Women's Press, New York

Chapter 4

Holborn, K (2018) ELIZABETH TAYLOR: An Elizabeth Taylor Biography, Independently Published

Ilube, T (2011) I'm good at failing [Blog], Tom Ilube, 4 June, available from: http://tomilube.blogspot.com/2011/ (archived at https://perma.cc/PG6V-R628) [last accessed: 13 January 2022]

Kubler-Ross, E (2014) On Death & Dying: What the Dying Have to Teach Doctors, Nurses, Clergy & Their Own Families, Scribner, New York

Lyons, A and Winter, L (2021) We all know how this ends: Lessons about life and living from working with death and dying, Green Tree, London

Nolen-Hoeksema, S (1991) Responses to depression and their effects on the duration of depressive episodes, Journal of Abnormal Psychology, (100), pp 569–582

Nolen-Hoeksema, S, Wisco, B and Lyubomirsky, S (2008) Rethinking Rumination, Perspectives on Psychological Science, [3] (5), pp 400–424

Shepard, D (2003) Learning from Business Failure: Propositions of Grief Recovery for the Self-Employed, The Academy of Management Review, [28] (2), pp 318–328

Worden, W (2003) Grief Counselling and Grief Therapy: A Handbook for the Mental Health Practitioner, Springer, New York

Chapter 5

BBC (2022) Elizabeth Holmes: Theranos founder convicted of fraud, BBC News, 4 January, available from: https://www.bbc.co.uk/news/world-us-canada-59734254 (archived at https://perma.cc/EK9Q-V4BV) [Last accessed: 14 January 2022]

Frankl, V (1959) Man's Search for Meaning: An Introduction to Logotherapy, 4th Edition, Beacon Press, Boston

Girard, K (2012) Why Most Leaders (Even Thomas Jefferson) Are Replaceable, Harvard Business School, 4 September, available from: https://hbswk.hbs.edu/item/7038.html (archived at https://perma.cc/9A34-E6W5) [Last accessed: 14 January 2022]

Godoy, J (2021) 'Failure is not a crime,' defense says in trial of Theranos founder Holmes, Reuters, 9 September, available from: https://www.reuters.com/business/healthcare-pharmaceuticals/fraud-trial-theranos-founder-elizabeth-holmes-set-begin-2021-09-08/ (archived at https://perma.cc/7UMA-NE2E) [Last accessed: 14 January 2022]

Green, B (2013) The man who turned rejection into a career, CNN, 4 August, available from: https://edition.cnn.com/2013/08/04/opinion/greene-rejection-success/index.html (archived at https://perma.cc/T7PT-QLVN) [Last accessed: 14 January 2022]

McCluskey, M (2021) Silicon Valley Investors Haven't Let the Theranos Scandal Change the Way They Do Business, Time, 9 September, available from: https://time.com/6092628/theranos-elizabeth-holmes-investors/ (archived at https://perma.cc/YR2S-8AVE) [Last accessed: 14 January 2022]

Mukunda, G (2012) *Indispensable: When Leaders Really Matter*, Harvard Business Review Press, Boston

Smith, D (2009) Driver wins £20,000 damages for stress of parking tickets, The Guardian, 8 February, available from: https://www.theguardian.com/uk/2009/feb/08/parking-fine-high-court-damages (archived at https://perma.cc/3BTT-3KDY) [Last accessed: 14 January 2022]

Chapter 6

Cabanas, E and Illouz, E (2019) *Manufacturing Happy Citizens: How the Science and Industry of Happiness Control our Lives,* Polity, Cambridge

Coyne, J (2015) Lucrative pseudoscience at the International Positive Psychology Association meeting, Coyne of the Realm, 15 July, available from: https://www.coyneoftherealm.com/2015/07/15/lucrative-pseudoscience-at-the-international-positive-psychology-association-meeting/ (archived at https://perma.cc/F8T4-GRES) [Last accessed: 14 January 2022]

Coyne, J (2019) "Positive psychology gives the impression you can be well and happ y just by thinking the right thoughts. It encourages a culture of blaming the victim," said professor Jim Coyne, a former colleague and fierce critic of Seligman. [Twitter] 20

November, available from: https://twitter.com/coyneoftherealm/status/1197259236016869378 (archived at https://perma.cc/88S3-9JYP) [Last accessed: 14 January 2022]

Latecki, B (2017) Pollyanna syndrome in psychotherapy-or pseudotherapy. Counseling, consoling or counterfeiting? *European Psychiatry*, [41], pp 777–778

Missimer, A (2020) Beat anxiety with curiosity, The movement paradigm, 18 February, available from: https://themovement paradigm.com/beat-anxiety-with-curiosity/ (archived at https://perma.cc/6BE2-ELW4) [Last accessed: 14 January 2022]

Oettingen, G and Wadden, T (1991) Expectation, fantasy, and weight loss: Is the impact of positive thinking always positive?, *Cognitive Therapy and Research*, [15], pp 167–175

Price, L (2021) 'I want to be remembered for doing epic stuff, not having breast cancer at 23', Metro, 19 August, available from: https://metro.co.uk/2021/08/19/i-want-to-be-remembered-for-doing-epic-stuff-not-having-cancer-at-23-15105160/ (archived at https://perma.cc/W9TN-AM95) [Last accessed: 14 January 2022]

Seligman, M (1998) President's Address from The APA 1998 Annual Report, app earing in the August, 1999 *American Psychologist*. available from: https://positivepsychologynews.com/ppnd_wp/wp-content/uploads/2018/04/APA-President-Address-1998.pdf (archived at https://perma.cc/TWQ2-N4UX) [Last accessed: 14 January 2022]

Stockdale, J (1995) *Thoughts of a Philosphical Fighter Pilot*, Hoover Institution Press, Stanford

Tenney, E, Logg, J and Moore, D (2015) (Too) optimistic about optimism: The belief that optimism improves performance, *Journal of Personality and Social Psychology*, [108] (3), pp 377–399

Chapter 7

Apted, M (1997) Inspirations, Argo Films, Clear Blue Sky Productions

Bridges, W (1995) *Managing Transitions: Making the Most of Change: Making the Most out of Change*, Nicholas Brealey Publishing, Boston, Massachusetts

Brown, B (2015) *Rising Strong: The Reckoning. the Rumble. the Revolution.*, Random House, New York

Conley, C (2018) *Wisdom at Work: The Making of a Modern Elder*, Portfolio Penguin, London

Gide, A (1927) *The Counterfeiters: A Novel*, Alfred A. Knopf, New York

Lewis, C (1920) *Alice's Adventures in Wonderland*, Macmillan, New York

Markel, H (2013) The real story behind penicillin, PBS News Hour, 27 September, available from: https://www.pbs.org/newshour/health/the-real-story-behind-the-worlds-first-antibiotic (archived at https://perma.cc/WD6E-MA7C) [Last accessed: 14 January 2022]

Missimer, A (2020) Beat anxiety with curiosity, The movement paradigm, 18 February, available from: https://themovementparadigm.com/beat-anxiety-with-curiosity/ (archived at https://perma.cc/6BE2-ELW4) [Last accessed: 14 January 2022]

Powell, C (2012) *It Worked for Me: In Life and Leadership*, Harper, New York

Saner, E (2021) Grayson Perry on art, cats – and the meaning of life: 'If you don't have self doubt, you're not trying hard enough', The Guardian, 9 November, available from: https://www.theguardian.com/artanddesign/2021/nov/09/grayson-perry-on-art-cats-and-meaning-of-life-if-you-dont-have-self-doubt-youre-not-trying-hard-enough (archived at https://perma.cc/5Y7A-5S54) [Last accessed: 14 January 2022]

Suzuki, S (1970) *Zen Mind, Beginners Mind*, Weatherhill, New York

Turner, V (1967) Betwixt and Between: The Liminal Period in Rites de Passage, in *The Forest of Symbols: Aspects of Ndembu Ritual*, Cornell University Press, Cornell

Chapter 8

Dishman, L (2018) Americans have been fighting for paid vacation for 100 years, Fast Company, 24th August, available from: https://www.fastcompany.com/90220227/the-history-of-how-we-got-paid-vacation-in-the-us (archived at https://perma.cc/8X92-EGUN) [Last accessed: 10 January 2022]

Gallup (2020) Gallup's Perspective on Employee Burnout: Causes and Cures [Online Report], available from: https://www.gallup.com/workplace/282659/employee-burnout-perspective-paper.aspx (archived at https://perma.cc/3AUE-VM9P) [Last accessed: 10 January 2022]

Hall, A (2019) Office Workers Only Take 16 Minutes Lunch Break, Study Suggests, The Independent, 19 June, available from: https://www.independent.co.uk/life-style/office-workers-lunch-break-poll-workplace-results-a8965551.html (archived at https://perma.cc/7SZ2-KAGW) [Last accessed: 10 January 2022]

HR News (2017) New survey finds Brits just won't stop working!, HR News, 29 June, available from: http://hrnews.co.uk/new-survey-finds-brits-just-wont-stop-working/ (archived at https://perma.cc/MWH8-8WBY) [Last accessed: 10 January 2022]

King James Bible (n.d.) King James Bible Online, available from: https://www.kingjamesbibleonline.org/ (archived at https://perma.cc/K5HL-UVV8) [Last accessed: 10 January 2022]

Office for National Statistics (2018) International comparisons of UK productivity (ICP), final estimates: 2016 [Online Report]. Available from:https://www.ons.gov.uk/economy/economicoutputand productivity/productivitymeasures/bulletins/internationalcomparis onsofproductivityfinalestimates/2016 (archived at https://perma.cc/83VK-X4FZ) [Last accessed: 10 January 2022]

Oxford Economics (2014) An Assessment of Paid Time Off in the U.S. [Online Report]. Available from: file:///C:/Users/GCollard/Downloads/US%20Paid%20%20Time%20Off.pdf [Last accessed: 10 January 2022]

Schwartz, T and McCarthy, C (2007) Manage Your Energy, Not Your Time, Harvard Business Review, available from: https://hbr.org/2007/10/manage-your-energy-not-your-time (archived at https://perma.cc/Y6EQ-SF4M) [Last accessed: 10 January 2022]

Weller, C (2019) Arianna Huffington On the Importance of 'Thrive Time', Your Brain at Work, 12 November, available from: https://neuroleadership.com/your-brain-at-work/arianna-huffington-nli-podcast-thrive-time#:~:text=Don't%20call%20it%20%E2%80%9Cdown,t%20be%20considered%20a%20luxury (archived at https://perma.cc/9CF6-X7KP) [Last accessed: 10 January 2022]

Chapter 9

Chang, J and Thompson, V (2012) Dolly Parton on Gay Rumors, Losing a Drag Queen Look-Alike Contest and New Memoir, ABC News, 26 November, available from: https://abcnews.go.com/Entertainment/dolly-parton-gay-rumors-losing-drag-queen-alike/story?id=17812138 (archived at https://perma.cc/6FFP-P7YQ) [Last accessed: 14 January 2022]

Connors, R and Smith T(2014) *The Wisdom of Oz: Using Personal Accountability to Succeed in Everything You Do,* Portfolio, New York

Dweck, C (2006) Mindset: The New Psychology of Success, Random House, New York

Ericsson, A and Harwell, K (2019) Deliberate Practice and Proposed Limits on the Effects of Practice on the Acquisition of Expert Performance: Why the Original Definition Matters and Recommendations for Future Research, *Frontiers in Psychology,* [10]

Global Entrepreneurship Monitor (2021) 2020/2021 Global Report [Online]. available from: https://www.gemconsortium.org/file/open?fileId=50691 (archived at https://perma.cc/KTS5-NC4B) [Last accessed: 14 January 2022]

Gov.uk (2019) Number of companies in the UK from 2018 to 2019, Gov.uk, 16 July, available from: https://www.gov.uk/government/news/uk-company-statistics-2018-to-2019 (archived at https://perma.cc/7Z46-J7C5) [Last accessed: 14 January 2022]

Kahneman, D and Tversky, A (1979) Prospect Theory: An Analysis of Decision under Risk, *Econometrica,* [47] (4), pp 263–291

Moss, C (2015) Anna Wintour thinks everyone should be fired once, Business Insider, 3 March, available from: https://www.businessinsider.com/anna-wintour-thinks-everyone-should-be-fired-once-2015-3?r=US&IR=T (archived at https://perma.cc/C4MA-K5DJ) [Last accessed: 14 January 2022]

Nielsen (2018) Setting the Record Straight on Innovation Failure [Online]. Available from: https://www.nielsen.com/wp-content/uploads/sites/3/2019/04/setting-the-record-straight-common-causes-of-innovation-failure-1.pdf (archived at https://perma.cc/AX38-QCU2) [Last accessed: 14 January 2022]

Nussbaum, A and Dweck, C (2008) Defensiveness Versus Remediation: Self-Theories and Modes of Self-Esteem Maintenance, *Personality and Social Psychology Bulletin,* [34] (5), pp 599–612

Office for National Statistics (2016) Divorces in England and Wales: 2016 [Online]. Available from: https://www.ons.gov.uk/peoplepopulationandcommunity/birthsdeathsandmarriages/divorce/bulletins/divorcesinenglandandwales/2016 (archived at https://perma.cc/EL53-Pp WC) [Last accessed: 14 January 2022]

Pretorius, M and Roux, I (2011) Successive failure, repeat entrepreneurship and no learning: A case study, *SA Journal of Human Resource Management,* [9] (1)

Qureshi, J (2020) Performance Psychologist Reveals the Secrets of Teamwork | Exclusive Q&A with Jamil Qureshi [YouTube]. 12 June. Available from: https://www.youtube.com/watch?v=N5opuVhY2mc&t=3s (archived at https://perma.cc/MYD6-6P3G) [Last accessed: 14 January 2022]

Qureshi, J (2021) The Psychology of Success Podcast, Episode 4, 23 April, available from: https://podcasts.apple.com/gb/podcast/jamil-qureshi-the-price-of-success-is-always-paid/id1561741449?i=1000518356596 (archived at https://perma.cc/A2VB-6CNZ) [Last accessed: 14 January 2022]

Chapter 10

Craig, A (2020) Discovery of 'thought worms' opens window to the mind, Queen's Gazette, 13 July, available from: https://www.queensu.ca/gazette/stories/discovery-thought-worms-opens-window-mind (archived at https://perma.cc/5867-CMLA) [Last accessed: 11 January 2022]

Foroux, D (2020) It's Okay To Change Your Mind, Medium, 14 April, available from: https://medium.com/darius-foroux/its-okay-to-change-your-mind-c4a0166b0a6d (archived at https://perma.cc/37GF-TY8D) [Last accessed: 11 January 2022]

Galbraith, J (1965) Came the Revolution; the General Theory of Employment, Interest, and Money, *The New York Times*, 16 May, available from: https://www.nytimes.com/1965/05/16/archives/came-the-revolution-the-general-theory-of-employment-interest-and.html (archived at https://perma.cc/V35Y-R4EZ) [Last accessed: 11 January 2022]

Keynes, J (1930) *A Treatise on Money*, Palgrave Macmillan, London

Keynes, J (1936) *The General Theory of Employment*, Interest and Money, Palgrave Macmillan, London

Monga, S (2020) Virat Kohli: My 'personality' is a 'representation' of 'new India', ESPN Cricinfo, 16 December, available from: https://www.espncricinfo.com/story/aus-vs-ind-2020-1st-test-pink-ball-adelaide-chappell-virat-kohli-my-personality-a-representation-of-new-india-1244080 (archived at https://perma.cc/H68C-X9X3) [Last accessed: 11 January 2022]

Obama, B (2019) [Online video]. Obama: I change my mind all the time based on facts, CNN, 28 April. available from: https://edition.cnn.com/videos/politics/2019/04/28/barack-obama-nelson-mandela-sot-vpx-ndwknd.cnn (archived at https://perma.cc/L9UB-ESVE) [Last accessed: 11 January 2022]

Pollan, M (2018) *How to Change Your Mind: The New Science of Psychedelics*, Allen Lane, New York

Williams, H (2018) The Physics of the Fosbury Flop, Stanford University, available from: http://large.stanford.edu/courses/2018/ph240/williams-h2/ (archived at https://perma.cc/PV4Q-CSSH) [Last accessed: 11 January 2022]

Chapter 11

Chang, C and Groeneveld, R (2018) Slowing down to speed up, McKinsey and Company, 23 March. Available from: https://www.mckinsey.com/business-functions/people-and-organizational-performance/our-insights/the-organization-blog/slowing-down-to-speed-up (archived at https://perma.cc/9E8X-J72S) [Last accessed: 26 October 2021]

Kahneman, D (2011) *Thinking, Fast and Slow,* Allen Lane, New York City

Kopka, U and Kruyt, M (2014) From bottom to top: Turning around the top team, McKinsey Quarterly, 1 November, available from: https://www.mckinsey.com/business-functions/people-and-organizational-performance/our-insights/from-bottom-to-top (archived at https://perma.cc/DH2E-4RQF) [Last accessed: 11 January 2022]

McKeever, V (2021) Matthew McConaughey explains how time off actually helped relaunch his career, CNBC, 18 June. Available from: https://www.cnbc.com/2021/06/18/matthew-mcconaughey-explains-how-time-off-helped-relaunch-his-career.html (archived at https://perma.cc/TLL9-DFER) [Last accessed; 26 October 2021]

Medina, J (2008) *Brain Rules: 12 Principles for Surviving and Thriving at Work, Home and School*, Pear Press, Seattle

Murray, R (2010) Foo Fighters On Their Band Name, Clash Music, 1 November. Available from: https://www.clashmusic.com/news/foo-fighters-on-their-band-name (archived at https://perma.cc/VV7Q-SVJV) [Last accessed: 26th October 2021]

Strauss, D (2018) There Are 2 Types of Leaders. 10 Questions to Find Out Which One You Are, Why physics has more to do with your leadership style than you think., INC, 22 February. Available from: https://www.inc.com/david-straus/newtonian-or-quantum-leader-10-questions-to-find-out-which-one-you-are.html (archived at https://perma.cc/TG9L-575Q) [Last accessed: 26 October 2021]

Chapter 12

de Berker, A, Rutledge, R, Mathys, C, Marshall, L, Cross, G, Dolan, R and Bestmann, S (2016) Computations of uncertainty mediate acute stress responses in humans, *Nature Communications*, [7], 10996

Grant, H and Goldhamer, T (2021) Our Brains Were Not Built for This Much Uncertainty, Harvard Business Review, 22 September, available from: https://hbr.org/2021/09/our-brains-were-not-built-for-this-much-uncertainty (archived at https://perma.cc/EV6Z-BREX) [Last accessed: 13 January 2022]

Heifetz, R and Linsky, M (2014) Adaptive Leadership: The Heifetz Collection (3 Items), *Harvard Business Review Press*, Boston

Kaplan, J and Stenberg, M (2020) Meet the astrology entrepreneurs who turned an awful 2020 into a boom for the $2.2 billion industry, Business Insider, 26 December, available from: https://www.businessinsider.com/astrology-industry-boomed-during-pandemic-online-entrepreneurs-2020-12?r=US&IR=T (archived at https://perma.cc/7L9F-WTGT) [Last accessed: 13 January 2022]

Kotter, J (2012) *Leading Change, With a New Preface by the Author*, Harvard Business Review Press, New York

Paulos, J (2004) *A Mathematician Plays the Stock Market*, Basic Books, New York

Chapter 13

Bostock, J (2014) Insights from Women at Cambridge [Online]. Available from: https://www.cam.ac.uk/system/files/the_meaning_of_success_final_revised_for_print_final.pdf (archived at https://perma.cc/KG4E-ZGY9) [Last accessed: 11 January 2022]

Drucker, P (1954) *The Practice of Management*, Harper & Row, New York

Musk, E (2017) 'The reality is great highs, terrible lows and unrelenting stress. Don't think people want to hear about the last two.' [Twitter], 30 July, available from: https://twitter.com/elonmusk/status/891710778205626368?lang=en (archived at https://perma.cc/CJ7B-ZVDS) [Last accessed 11 January 2022]

Chapter 14

Edmondson, A (2018) *The Fearless Organization: Creating Psychological Safety in the Workplace for Learning, Innovation, and Growth*, Wiley, Hoboken

Gallagher, N (2017) *The Airbnb Story: How Three Ordinary Guys Disrupted an Industry, Made Billions . . . and Created Plenty of Controversy*, Harper Business, New York

Punks with Purpose (2021) An Open Letter to BrewDog, Punks with Purpose, 9 June, available from: https://www.punkswithpurpose.org/dearbrewdog/ (archived at https://perma.cc/KA6J-ZA8M) [Last accessed: 13 January 2022]

Rahim, A (2010) *Managing Conflict in Organizations*, Routledge, London and New York

Scott, K (2017) *Radical Candor: Be a Kick-Ass Boss Without Losing Your Humanity*, St. Martin's Press, New York

UK Violence Intervention and Prevention Centre, The Four Basic Styles of Communication [Online]. Available from: https://www.uky.edu/hr/sites/www.uky.edu.hr/files/wellness/images/Conf14_FourCommStyles.pdf (archived at https://perma.cc/L2BG-GC9P) [Last accessed: 13 January 2022]

Chapter 15

Aristotle (2004), The Nicomachean Ethics (Penguin Classics), Thomson, H (tr), Penguin Classics, London

Aronson, E, Willerman, B and Floyd, J (1966) The effect of a pratfall on increasing interpersonal attractiveness, *Psychonomic Science*, [**4**], pp 227–228

Brown, H (2022) Herzon Brown, Prince's Trust, Success Stories, available from: https://www.princes-trust.org.uk/about-the-trust/success-stories/hezron-brown (archived at https://perma.cc/7Z9B-4Z9D) [Last accessed: 11 January 2022]

Chapter 16

Obama, B (2009) Speech, Wakefield High School [YouTube], 15 September, available from: https://www.youtube.com/watch?v=-uWxdTxBi2g (archived at https://perma.cc/96SD-JA7T) [Last accessed: 11 January 2022]

Flynn, F and Lake, V (2008) "If you need help, just ask": Underestimating compliance with direct requests for help, *Journal of Personality and Social Psychology*, [**95**] (1), pp 128–143

Rigoglioso, M (2008) Studies show people underestimate the willingness of others to help them out, Stanford News, 6 August, available from: https://news.stanford.edu/news/2008/august6/justask-080608.html (archived at https://perma.cc/6LXL-7Z74) [Last accessed: 11 January 2022]

Chapter 17

Bennett, K (2015) Emotional and Personal Resilience Through Life [Online]. Available from: https://assets.publishing.service.gov.uk/government/uploads/system/uploads/attachment_data/file/456126/gs-15-19-future-ageing-emotional-personal-resilience-er04.pdf (archived at https://perma.cc/UAA6-CNVW) [Last accessed: 23 December 2021]

Duckworth, A (2017) *Grit: Why Passion and Resilience are the Secrets to Success*, Vermillion, London

Limbach, P and Sonnenburg F (2015) Does CEO Fitness Matter? CFR Working Paper NO. 14-12, Centre for Financial Research, available from: https://www.econstor.eu/bitstream10419/123715/1/841379122.pdf (archived at https://perma.cc/9WUG-4CHD) [Last accessed: 23 December 2021]

Zimmerman, E (2020) What Makes Some People More Resilient Than Others, The New York Times, 18 June, available from: https://www.nytimes.com/2020/06/18/health/resilience-relationships-trauma.html (archived at https://perma.cc/H5CP-QDUZ) [Last accessed: 23 December 2021]

Chapter 18

Burns, J (2012) 'Failure week' at top girls' school to build resilience, BBC News, 5 February, available from: https://www.bbc.co.uk/news/education-16879336 (archived at https://perma.cc/DEZ8-W2BB) [Last accessed: 11 January 2022]

Dell Technologies (2018) Realizing 2030: A Divided Vision of the Future [Online Report]. Available from: https://www.dell technologies.com/content/dam/delltechnologies/assets/perspec tives/2030/pdf/Realizing-2030-A-Divided-Vision-of-the-Future-Summary.pdf (archived at https://perma.cc/4A3D-VDS6) [Last accessed: 11 January 2022]

Dondi, M, Klier, J, Panier, F and Schubert, J (2021) Defining the skills citizens will need in the future world of work, McKinsey and Company, 25 June, available from: https://www.mckinsey.com/ industries/public-and-social-sector/our-insights/defining-the-skills-citizens-will-need-in-the-future-world-of-work (archived at https://perma.cc/9YJV-33HS) [Last accessed: 11 January 2022]

Dweck, C (2006) Mindset: The New Psychology of Success, Random House, New York

Dweck, C (2014) The power of believing that you can improve [TED Talk]. Available from: https://www.ted.com/talks/carol_dweck_ the_power_of_believing_that_you_can_improve?language=en (archived at https://perma.cc/K6KP-5VVT) [Last accessed: 11 January 2022]

Fenton, C (2019) Playful Curiosity: A Manifesto for Reinventing Education, Nielson

McKinsey & Company (2022) Future of Work, available from: https://www.mckinsey.com/featured-insights/future-of-work (archived at https://perma.cc/9VT6-6V4Q) [Last accessed: 11 January 2022]

Mueller, C and Dweck, C (1998) Praise for intelligence can undermine children's motivation and performance, Journal of Personality and Social Psychology, [75] (1), pp 33–52

re:Work (2022) re:Work with Google [Online]. Available from: https://rework.withgoogle.com/print/guides/5721312655835136/ (archived at https://perma.cc/ZK6H-JE2S) [Last accessed: 11 January 2022]

Robinson, K (2006) Do schools kill creativity? [TED Talk], February. Available from: https://www.ted.com/talks/sir_ken_robinson_do_schools_kill_creativity (archived at https://perma.cc/849F-S248) [Last accessed: 11 January 2022]

Index